100

HISPANIC-AMERICANS

WHO SHAPED AMERICAN HISTORY

Rick Laezman

A Bluewood Book

This edition produced and published
by Bluewood Books
A Division of The Siyeh Group, Inc.,
P.O. Box 689
San Mateo, CA 94401

ISBN 0-912517-47-6

Printed in U.S.A.
10, 9, 8, 7, 6, 5, 4, 3, 2, 1

Editor: Tony Napoli
Editorial Assistance: Marilyn Harper
Indexer: Barbara Cross
Designer: Kevin Harris

Key to cover illustration: Clockwise,
starting from the top left: Juan Ponce
de Leon, Romana Acosta Banuelos,
Father Junipero Serra, Carmen
Miranda, Dolores Huerta, Edward
James Olmos, Lauro F. Cavazos, and
Cesar Chavez in the center.

About the Author:
Rick Laezman is a freelance
writer. This is Mr. Laezman's first
book. He contributes regularly to
national magazines, such as *Latino
Leaders* and *Hispanic Business*. He
lives in Los Angeles, California.

Picture Acknowledgements:
All images and photos from the
Bluewood Archives; Library of
Congress; National Archives;
National Portrait Gallery; San Mateo
Public Library; and the White House
with the following exceptions: 48,
64: American Ballet Theater; 80:
American Broadcasting Company;
52: Romana Acosta Banuelos; 18,
20: California Department of Parks &
Recreation; 55: Lauro F. Cavazos;
65: Coca-Cola Company; 47:
Columbia Pictures Television; 67:
Oscar de la Renta; 43: Desilu
Productions; 94: Farrar Straus
Giroux; 26: Harvard University; 25:
Institute of Puerto Rican Culture; 41:
Institute of Texas Cultures of San
Antonio; 28: La Opinion; 33: Metro-
Goldwyn-Mayer; 72: Miami-Dade
Tourism; 103: NASA; 49: Antonia
Pantoja; 39, 42, 44, 54, 56, 60,
62, 66, 73, 74, 76, 77, 79, 82, 86,
87, 88, 89, 90, 91, 93, 100, 102,
104, 107: George Rodriguez; 36:
20th Century Fox; 21, 29, 34, 45,
50, 53, 57, 58, 59, 61, 63, 68, 69,
70, 71, 75, 78, 81, 83, 84, 85, 92,
95, 97, 98, 99, 105, 106: Zimou
Larry Tan; 38: Texas A&M University;
19: Texas State Library; 40, 96: U.S.
House of Representatives; 32:
University of Texas

TABLE OF CONTENTS

1.   2. 3.   4.   5. 6.   7.   8.   9.   10. 14.   11. 15.   12.   13.   16.   17.   18.   19.   20.   21.   22.   23.   24.   25.   26.

1450   **1900**

TABLE OF CONTENTS

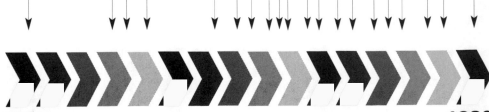

1901   1930

TABLE OF CONTENTS

58.
59.
60.   61.   62.
63.
64.
65.   66.
67.
68.   69.
70.
71.   74.
72.   75.
73.   76.
77.

1931

1945

TABLE OF CONTENTS

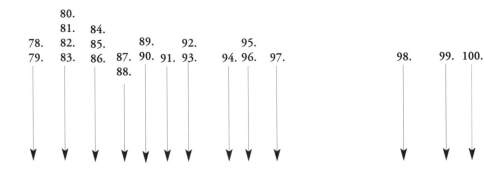

1946   1975

INTRODUCTION

In the late 20th and early 21st centuries, the population of Hispanics in the United States surged to unprecedented numbers, and the country became more aware of their powerful influence on American culture and society. However, Hispanic influence is not a new phenomenon. For more than 500 years, descendants of the Spanish-speaking world have been changing the course of United States history.

One of the first Spanish explorers to take up residence in the New World, Juan Ponce de León is best known for his failed search for the mythical fountain of youth. More importantly, he was the first European to explore the mainland of what would become the United States, and his explorations paved the way for future settlement of the country.

Representatives of the Catholic Church routinely accompanied Spanish explorers such as Ponce de León. Their job was to provide religious services to the colonists and help "civilize" the natives. The most well known of these religious pioneers, Father Junipero Serra, was one of the first Europeans to set foot on present-day California. He established nearly a dozen Catholic missions there, in his tireless effort to bring Christianity to the natives.

Of course, Hispanics have influenced American life in many ways besides exploration and conquest. The Cuban-born doctors, Carlos Juan Finlay and Juan Guiteras, proposed daring new theories, which eventually led to the eradication of the deadly disease, yellow fever. When the Spanish architect Rafael Guastavino came to America, he brought with him a centuries-old architectural technique known as the Catalan vault, which became immensely popular on the East Coast at the turn of the 20th century.

Sadly, in spite of their varied and significant contributions, Hispanics have also faced discrimination and injustice in the United States. Consequently, many Hispanic-Americans who influenced American history have made the greatest contribution on the front lines of the battle against racial prejudice. The most well known and revered of all Hispanic civil rights leaders, César Chávez, called attention to the plight of American farm workers. He formed the United Farmworkers Union to improve their living and working conditions, and his efforts transformed him into an icon of the Mexican-American (Chicano) civil rights movement.

Hispanic-Americans have also contributed greatly to American culture. In the mid-20th century, bandleaders such as Xavier Cugat and Tito Puente popularized Latin dance songs like the rumba and the cha-cha. Entertainers of a later generation, such as Gloria Estefan and Selena, carried on the tradition by introducing American audiences to a new brand of music infused with Latin sounds. And athletes such as Roberto Clemente, Lee Trevino, and Nancy Lopez achieved great success and popularity in the highly competitive world of professional sports.

Hispanic-American politicians have also influenced American civic life. Leaders such as Lauro Cavazos, Federico Peña, and Henry Cisneros have helped shaped the national dialogue on education, transportation, and housing.

The "American dream" has touched countless Hispanic-Americans over the years. Ignacio Lozano founded a small fledgling Spanish-language newspaper in Los Angeles in the 1920's. Seventy-five years later, *La Opinión*, still owned and operated by the Lozano family, was the mostly widely read Spanish-language newspaper in the United States. Antonia Novello overcame childhood illness growing up in Puerto Rico during the 1940s and 50s, became a physician in America, and rose to be appointed surgeon general of the United States. And, during the 1970s and 80s, Roberto Goizueta climbed the ranks of Coca Cola, from a staff chemist to president and C.E.O., and transformed the beverage company into an international powerhouse.

These are only a few of the 100 men and women whose stories are contained in this book— Hispanic-Americans who have helped shaped U.S. history. As their numbers grow, their contributions gain more recognition, and they will continue to leave their mark as the country moves well into the 21st century.

1. Juan Ponce de León
(1460–1521)

Born in Valladolid, Spain, **Juan Ponce de León** first called attention to himself as a soldier. As a captain in the nobleman Don Pedro Nunez de Guzman's private army, he so impressed King Ferdinand with his valor that the king knighted him on the field at the Battle of Toro.

Ponce de León joined **Christopher Columbus's** second journey to the Americas in 1493. During the journey, Ponce de León became the first man of European descent to set foot on what would later be known as **Puerto Rico** when his vessel had to stop on the then unknown island to look for water.

On a subsequent trip in 1502, Ponce de León led the war against the native Higuey tribe on the island of **Hispaniola** (present-day Haiti). After

Ponce de León

two years, the natives were defeated, and Ponce de León was promoted to the rank of lieutenant. In 1509, he was appointed governor of San Juan Bautista (present-day Puerto Rico) in recognition of his successful campaign against the natives on that island.

In 1512, political infighting with the Columbus family forced Ponce de León out of the governorship. He subsequently embarked on an exploration to the island of Bimini to find riches, regain his glory, and discover a rumored **Fountain of Youth**. He led a team of ships through the Bahamas and eventually came to **Florida**. Although they believed they were on an island, there his party planted the Spanish flag for the first time on the soil of mainland North America. Because the landing took place on Easter Sunday, during the time of the calendar the church called Pascua Florida, and because the land contained such lush greenery, Ponce de León named the area Florida, the Land of Flowers.

Evading hostile natives on shore, the men spent most of the time navigating the coast of Florida, as opposed to establishing any permanent settlements or exploring inland. Their activities represented the first documented navigation of the Florida peninsula. Also during the expedition, Ponce de León's pilot, Antonio de Alaminos, discovered the Gulf Stream.

Although the trip failed to achieve its original goals, the knowledge gained on this historic voyage triggered a wave of future explorations, which paved the way for the eventual settlement by Europeans of mainland North America.

Ponce de León concluded his journey and returned to Puerto Rico, where he was reinstated as governor in 1514, but he could not resist the allure of Florida. In 1521, he returned there to establish a permanent settlement. However, he again encountered hostile natives when he landed at Charlotte Harbor. He took a poison arrow in the leg and retreated to Havana, where he died several days later.

2. Pedro Menendez de Avilés
(1519–1574)

Pedro Menendez de Avilés was possessed by a need to sail the world at an early age. Born in Avilés, Spain, he ran away from home and enlisted as a cabin boy on a ship in Santander Harbor at the age of 14.

Menendez then embarked on a successful naval career in service to the Spanish crown. He distinguished himself with his knowledge of routes to the **West Indies**, helping Spain design and implement a system of routes for shipping to and from the islands, safe from marauding pirates and other enemies.

In 1561, Menendez was rewarded with an appointment as captain general of the Armada de la Carrera de Indies, the largest fleet ever to leave Spain, with 49 ships. He continued to exploit his knowledge of the West Indies, advising the Spanish royalty on the development of trade regulations there, and on the fortifications of important harbors such as Santa Domingo, San Juan de Puerto Rico, Havana, and Cartagena. Because of his experience in this area, he was appointed governor of Cuba and commander of Florida in 1567.

Menendez played an important role in the opening of the Indies as a trade route. Under his leadership, the islands were developed and exploited to suit the needs of the Spanish crown and the merchant ships that served it.

In 1567, Menendez again made an important contribution to the colonization of North America. He founded the first permanent settlement of European inhabitants on the mainland, at **St. Augustine,** Florida. The settlement was a strategic post for Spain to defend its holdings in Florida, but more importantly, it became an entry point for migration into the mainland.

In addition to acquiring settlers, St. Augustine also served as an entry point for Jesuit missionaries along the Atlantic coast. Only a small number of monks were a part of the initial settlement, but their numbers grew as they established missions, evangelized to the natives, and attended to the religious

Pedro Menendez de Avilés

needs of European settlers. Eventually, the Catholic Church established more than 100 missions in Florida.

The settlement of St. Augustine also represented the introduction of a Spanish system of local government. This included an elected town council, elected mayor, open town meetings, and other characteristics of Spanish democracy, all of which became common features in towns and municipalities in the United States.

Menendez was not content with Florida. His ambitions extended all the way to Canada. However, in 1567 he was recalled to Spain to lead an invasion of England. He died before the invasion took place.

Juan de Oñate
(1550–1630)

More than any other figure in the era of Spanish colonization, **Juan de Oñate** was personally responsible for the introduction of Hispanic culture into the southwestern United States.

Oñate was born to a wealthy mining family in Zacatecas, Mexico. He married the great-grand-daughter of the Aztec emperor **Montezuma**. Like most Spanish colonizers, he had a hunger for exploration, fueled by a lust for riches.

In 1595, Oñate was granted a charter from the Spanish king to explore and colonize the area known as **Nuevo Mexico** (New Mexico). Eventually, the Spanish colony of New Spain would extend to encompass what are now the American Southwest, Mexico, Central America, the West Indies, and the Philippines.

Three years later, Oñate departed with more than 400 men and their families. They traveled north along the valley of the Rio Grande River, establishing a minor post along the way, which later became **El Paso, Texas**. From El Paso, the group continued north into Pueblo Indian territory. They arrived at a place called Caypa and established a settlement there. Oñate renamed it **San Juan de los**

Caballeros. It was the first town established by Europeans in the American Southwest.

Oñate served as the governor of New Mexico under the Spanish crown for several years, and his reign was very controversial. Many people claimed he was motivated primarily by a desire to discover riches, and he was also accused of severely brutalizing the natives. Still, Oñate left an important legacy. After several failed journeys away from San Juan de los Caballeros in search of silver, Oñate discovered a route through Zuni and Hopi Indian country to the Colorado and Gila rivers and ultimately to the Gulf of California, then known as the South Sea.

Included in Oñate's original search party were ten **Franciscans**, who remained after Oñate departed from the territory several years later. The Franciscans immediately began preaching to the natives. They built a church, and by 1630 they had established 25 missions among the Pueblo Indians.

Oñate's party also brought with it over 11,000 head of stock to support the silver mining industry. The stock included more than 4,000 churros, or shaggy sheep, from the Old World, which easily acclimated to the climate of the region. The sheep became an important part of the livestock industry that later developed in New Mexico and the neighboring Great Plains states.

In 1607, having spent all of his personal wealth colonizing New Mexico, Oñate resigned his governorship and returned to Mexico. He was later convicted of charges of brutality against the natives and colonizers. He spent much of the rest of his life trying to clear his name in Mexico and in Spain, where he died.

A Zuni pueblo, New Mexico

4. Junipero Serra
(1713–1784)

Father **Junipero Serra** came to New Spain to civilize the Indians. He traveled over 10,000 miles in **Mexico** and what would later become **California**, mostly by foot, and converted nearly 6,800 natives. The network of missions he helped establish laid the groundwork for the Spanish colonization of California, and had a profound impact on the history of the region.

Miguel José Serra was born in the town of Petra on the Spanish island of Majorca. He attended the university in Palma, the capital of Majorca, where he graduated at the age of 16. After the university, he joined the **Catholic Order of Saint Francis**, and was ordained as a priest after eight years of study. While studying at the Order, he took the name Junipero, after one of Saint Francis's most devoted followers.

Serra taught philosophy at the university in Palma for many years. In 1749, he left Spain and traveled with the Franciscan missionaries to Mexico. He disembarked at Veracruz, and walked the remaining distance to the College of San Fernando in Mexico City. It was the first of many long journeys by foot.

For many years, Serra traversed Mexico by foot, visiting various missions, teaching the Indians, and converting them to Christianity. In 1768, he was placed in charge of all the missions on the peninsula of Baja (Lower) California.

Spain faced mounting competition from Russia and Great Britain in colonizing the lands north of Baja in **Alta (Upper) California**. In 1769, the Spanish government assigned a team of explorers and missionaries to colonize the land, and Serra was placed in charge of establishing the missions during the expedition.

Serra traveled to Alta California by foot, while supply ships paralleled his route by sea.

Father Junipero Serra

In July, they met at the Bay of **San Diego**. Serra built his **first mission** there, a chapel, out of tree branches.

The next year, the expedition traveled to **Monterey**, where Serra built a second mission. The third mission followed soon after, in Carmel. Serra made his permanent home in Carmel, but he continued to travel up and down Alta California, administering to the existing missions and building new ones.

By 1774, Serra had built five more missions along a route that later became known as El Camino Real, or The King's Highway. By the time of his death, he had established a total of nine missions. Many California cities bear the names of the original missions that were founded there, such as San Luis Obispo, San Juan Capistrano, Santa Clara, San Gabriel, and San Francisco. The Franciscan order continued to proselytize to the Indians after Serra's death, establishing a total of 21 missions in Alta California.

Born in Sonora, Mexico, the son of a Spanish official, **Juan Bautista de Anza** played an important role in the conquest and settlement of early **California.**

In the late 18th century, the Spanish government aggressively protected and expanded its land holdings in the colony of **New Spain**, which included the lands of California. Complicating this ambitious agenda, at this time all travel from Mexico to Alta California was done by sea.

In 1773, Juan Bautista de Anza was serving as the commander of the Spanish forces in Tubac, in northern Mexico. That year the Spanish viceroy of

Juan Bautista de Anza

New Spain, Don **Antonio María Bucardi,** summoned de Anza to embark on a journey. He directed de Anza to find a passable overland route from Mexico to the northernmost presidio of California, at **Monterey.**

In January 1774, de Anza embarked on a exploratory expedition with **Pedro de Garcés,** a Franciscan missionary, as his traveling companion. They departed from Tubac and proceeded across the Sonoran Desert. They reached the junction of the Gila and Colorado rivers, where they established good relations with Chief Palma of the Yuma Indians. After their stop, they continued their journey north.

In March, de Anza and de Garcés reached Mission San Gabriel, located near present-day **Los Angeles**. After a brief stop to rest and replenish supplies, they continued on to

Monterey, several hundred miles to the north.

When de Anza reached Monterey, he stayed long enough to reinforce the mission there and build a presidio. He also ventured north to explore the area around **San Francisco Bay**.

Eventually, de Anza returned to Mexico City to report to the viceroy about the journey. Bucardi congratulated him on his successful mission and, in particular, for establishing the coveted land route to Alta California. He then gave de Anza a second assignment.

In October 1775, de Anza led a team of 240 settlers on a journey, over the land route he had established, to San Francisco. They brought with them more than 700 horses, 350 cattle, and enough provisions to establish a self-sustaining presidio.

Almost a year later, in 1776, de Anza founded the presidio of San Francisco. The fort represented the northernmost outpost of New Spain. It reinforced the northern border of the colony, which deterred British and Russian advances on the territory. Like all the other presidios in New Spain, it also protected and enforced the will of the missions—to preach Christianity, in many cases forcefully, to the Native Americans.

De Anza eventually returned to Mexico City and was later appointed governor of New Mexico.

6. Bernardo de Gálvez
(1746–1786)

As the colonial governor of **Spanish Louisiana, Bernardo de Gálvez** secretly sided with the American colonists during the **Revolutionary War** and used his power to help them defeat the British.

Gálvez was born in Spain, near the city of Málaga, and followed the paths of his father and uncle, both of whom had been high-ranking government officials. At the age of 16, he enlisted in the army, where he distinguished himself during many years of service. He traveled the world, defending the Spanish crown in Africa, Europe, and North America.

Gálvez first visited New Spain (present-day Mexico) at the age of 19, with his uncle, José de Gálvez, who held the powerful post of inspector general there. The young man was not to see the colony again for 12 years.

Then, in January 1777, after he had established a successful military career, he returned as the newly appointed governor of Spanish Louisiana. Later that year, he married Felicite Destrehan, the widowed daughter of a prominent French Creole family. The marriage gained him the affection and loyalty of the native Creole population of **New Orleans**. During his early months as governor, Gálvez also had his forces set up a settlement on an island off the coast of Texas. Originally named Gálvez, it later became known as **Galveston**.

Spain was officially neutral at the beginning of the American War of Independence. However, Spanish officials saw the conflict as an opportunity to eliminate British influence from the continent, and they secretly aided the Americans.

Gálvez sent covert shipments of supplies up the Mississippi River to the Americans who were fighting in the remote, isolated territories north of Louisiana. When American ships docked in New Orleans, he confiscated them in plain sight of British observers. Then he secretly allowed them to go free. At the same time, Gálvez made it difficult for the British to use the port for their shipments. He also obtained loans for the Americans from the Spanish government.

Bernardo de Gálvez

In 1779, when Spain declared war on Britain, Gálvez called on his military expertise. In numerous battles, he reclaimed for Spain all of the major ports along the Gulf of Mexico, such as Baton Rouge, Mobile, and Pensacola, which the British had taken in the previous decade. If not for Gálvez, the British would have launched attacks against the Americans from these ports.

After the war, Gálvez returned to Louisiana, with the new title of Count. He brought in food and cattle and encouraged English-speaking colonists to move there and become Spanish citizens.

In 1785, Gálvez was appointed viceroy of New Spain, a post held previously by his father. A year later, he became seriously ill with a fever and died.

7. Manuel Lisa
(1772–1820)

During the peak of his career, **Manuel Lisa** was the most influential person on the Western frontier. Of Spanish descent, he was born in New Orleans, Louisiana. He became involved in the **fur trade** as a teenager, and in 1799, he moved to St. Louis where he began to build a thriving business.

Manuel Lisa

Lisa started to explore the uncharted territories surrounding the upper Missouri River and established several trading posts along the way. Within a few years, he had established the **Missouri Fur Company** with other traders, including the famous American **William Clark** and the Frenchman **Pierre Chouteau**.

Lisa's success was due largely to the strong relationships he cultivated with the Native Americans in the region. For example, he had strong ties with the Osage, Omaha, and Pawnee Indians. His relationships with the Indians were helpful not only to his trading business, but to the United States government. He became an Indian agent, and is credited with converting the Sioux Indians from bitter enemies to loyal allies. When the United States fought the British in the **War of 1812**, Lisa used his friendships to win the loyalty of many of the Indian tribes.

After the United States made the famous Louisiana Purchase in 1803, and Lewis and Clark made their historic expedition, Lisa saw great potential in using St. Louis as an outpost for trade with the Indians to the west and the Spaniards in New Mexico. However, Governor Wilkinson of Upper Louisiana forbade him from executing his plan, perhaps fearing Lisa's growing power and wealth. Wilkinson's motives may have also been political, since the United States coveted the Spanish territories, and the government did not want to do anything to aid the Spaniards there.

Undaunted, Lisa traveled north. He traded with the Missouri Indians, and he opened forts (trading posts) in the region. He established **Fort Raymond** at the mouth of the Bighorn River, where he traded with the Crow Indians, as well as **Manuel's Fort,** on the Yellowstone River. This location served as a starting point for exploration parties into the remote regions that later became the state of **Montana**.

In 1812, Lisa built **Fort Lisa** ten miles north of present-day Omaha, Nebraska. It became the most important trading post on the Missouri River for several years, as the Missouri Fur Company grew into a trading empire. The company had more than 100 employees, and it handled more than $600,000 worth of furs and skins during its peak years. Lisa and his company contributed so significantly to the early trade and settlement of Nebraska, he is known there as the **"Founder of Old Nebraska."**

14

8. Antonio José Martínez
(1793 –1867)

A controversial figure within the Catholic Church, Father **Antonio José Martínez** fought his entire adult life for the rights of people whose plight aroused his passion—Mexicans, Indians, slaves, and the poor in New Mexico.

Martínez was born in the village of Abiquiu and was raised in the town of **Taos,** in the territory of **Nuevo Mexico** (New Mexico), which was then part of Mexico. He married at the age of 19, but his wife died during childbirth. The daughter that she gave birth to died some time later.

Despondent, Martínez entered a seminary. He was ordained a few years later and, in 1826, was appointed rector of the parish in his hometown of Taos, where he remained the rest of his life.

Martínez quickly established himself as a civic leader and a champion of nuevo mexicanos (New Mexicans of Mexican descent). He established a preparatory school, seminary, and college at his rectory, which catered to the brightest students in the area. He used much of the wealth that he inherited from his father to acquire scarce educational materials for his poor students. In particular, he bought the first printing press to be brought west of the Mississippi River, and he used it to publish religious and nonreligious texts.

Martínez studied law and became a deputy in the territorial legislature, becoming one of its most prominent members. He spoke out against unpopular taxes, and his remarks were believed to have caused an uprising against the Mexican government in 1837. He was also accused of inciting an Indian rebellion the following year.

Martínez was a staunch foe of the encroachment of Anglo culture. He denounced the slaughter of bison and the issuing of large land grants to U.S. settlers. His anti-American sentiments led to accusations that he also incited insurrections against U.S. forces, although no evidence was ever produced to confirm the allegations.

Martínez continued his involvement in politics after the United States won the war with Mexico in 1848, and took over the territory of Nuevo Mexico. He actively participated in the New Mexico statehood convention and went on to serve in the new state assembly, eventually becoming its president. He also became an **abolitionist** and an advocate for the rights of Native Americans.

In the 1850s, Martínez became involved in a dispute with his superior, the new bishop Jean Baptiste Lamy, a Frenchman who believed all Mexicans needed to be more rigidly civilized. The clash led to Martínez's excommunication from the Catholic Church, but he ignored the punishment and continued to preach to his own followers until his death.

Antonio José Martínez

9. Maria Gertrudes Barceló
(1800–1852)

Maria Gertrudes Barceló earned her fame during an era when women were not expected to make a name for themselves. Born in Sonora, Mexico to a privileged, well-educated family, she moved with her family in 1820 to the village of Valencia, **New Mexico** after Mexico won its independence from Spain.

In 1823, Barceló married, but in the first of many daring acts of independence, she insisted on retaining her maiden name. She also refused to relinquish to her husband either her right to make contracts or the deeds to her property, both of which were expected of women in those days. Within a few years, Barceló committed another brazen act by leaving her failing marriage and going to **Santa Fe** to pursue financial opportunities.

In 1825, Barceló began working as a dealer of the Mexican game of chance known as **monte bank**, which was popular with the

Maria Gertrudes Barceló

miners in the Ortiz Mountains. She soon became the most skilled dealer in town.

After several years, Barceló saved up enough money to purchase her own monte bank casino, which in a short period of time became one of the most popular casinos in Santa Fe. It was favored by the city's high society, whose members were drawn to its ornate interior with glass mirrors and plush carpets. More importantly, they were drawn to the charm and beauty of the hostess.

Barceló became one of the wealthiest people—man or woman—in the city of Santa Fe. She was popular with the ruling Mexican elite and was reputed at one time to be romantically involved with the governor of New Mexico, **Manuel Armijo**. Some people believed she was the true brains and power behind the governor's administration.

More than an independent-minded and ambitious woman, Barceló was also an opportunist who played both sides to her advantage. She advised the military of both countries during the **Mexican-American War**, and soldiers from both sides came to her casino to dance, gamble, drink, and talk politics.

In the 1840s, Barceló invested much of her considerable wealth in the United States. After America won the Mexican-American War, and occupied New Mexico, she became a valuable friend to the occupiers. She passed along important information regarding possible insurrections, and she provided loans to the U.S. forces for supplies. True to character, one of her loans included terms that required one of the American officers to escort her to a military ball.

In her final act of drama and self-promotion, Barceló arranged her own funeral. She made sure that it would be one of the most ornate and expensive funerals in the history of Santa Fe.

10. David Farragut
(1801–1870)

James Glasgow Farragut was born into a family of career soldiers dating back centuries. Pedro Farragut was a high-ranking officer in the 13th century army of Spain's King James I. Farragut's father, Jorge, immigrated to North America from Spain and fought as a lieutenant in the U.S. Navy during the Revolutionary War.

Farragut was born on the family farm at Campbell's Station, Tennessee. His mother died of yellow fever when he was young. After her death, Jorge Farragut parceled out all but one of his sons to be cared for temporarily by other families. A family friend, naval officer **David Porter Jr.**, offered to look after one of the sons as a favor to Jorge, who years before had cared for Porter's father on his death bed. As part of the offer, Porter also agreed to give the boy a proper naval officer's upbringing. James Farragut enthusiastically volunteered to go with the Porters. He embraced his new family and ultimately changed his name to David, in honor of his adoptive father.

Before he was even a teenager, David Farragut became a midshipman on Porter's ship, where he saw combat against the British in the **War of 1812**. As a young officer, he later saw action against pirates in the West Indies, and during the 1840s, he served in the war against Mexico.

In the 1860s, as a 60-year-old captain, Farragut joined the Union cause in the **Civil War**. In 1862, he commanded the squadron that captured the city of **New Orleans**, a vital Confederate port. He earned the nickname **"Old Salamander"** for the way he slipped past canon fire in that battle. Later, he cut off **Vicksburg**, which enabled General Ulysses S. Grant to conquer that city. For these victories, which gave the Union complete control of the Mississippi River, President Abraham Lincoln promoted Farragut to rear admiral.

Admiral David Farragut

In 1864, Farragut initiated a blockade of the city of **Mobile** on the Gulf of Mexico. At the time, Mobile was protected by hundreds of torpedo mines. The floating gunpowder bombs would explode when struck by a ship, and they destroyed one of the armored vessels in Farragut's fleet. When some of the other ships in the fleet began to back out of the channel, Farragut shouted a famous rallying cry, "Damn the torpedoes! Full speed ahead!" The fleet regrouped, entered the harbor without further incident, and eventually captured the city.

Farragut became an instant hero, and was later promoted to the position of full admiral, the first person ever to hold that title. He died of a heart attack while inspecting a naval base in New Hampshire in 1870.

11. Pio de Jesus Pico
(1801–1894)

As the last Mexican governor of **California**, **Pio de Jesus Pico** completed the secularization of the Catholic missions and authorized numerous land grants on the eve of the **Mexican-American War**.

Pico's ethnic heritage was a mix of African, Native American, Hispanic, and European ancestry. The fourth of ten children, he was born on the San Gabriel Mission to one of California's pioneering families. His grandfather, father, and other family members had come to San Francisco on the famous expedition led by **Juan Bautista de Anza** (see no. 5) in 1776.

Pio de Jesus Pico

While in office, Pico presided over the final secularization of the missions and the disbursement of their vast land holdings. The missions had been an important element of the Spanish colonization of the region, but were disbanded by Mexico after it won its independence from Spain. The sale of the last remaining mission lands signified the end of an era. Pico also made large grants of land in an attempt to counter the immigration of American settlers; however, his actions were criticized for being favorable to friends and allies.

Pico was raised in San Diego, and he began his career in politics there in 1826, as clerk of a court-martial. Two years later, he was elected to the territorial *diputacion*, the territorial legislature of Alta, or Upper, California, as the area was then known. In 1831, Pico led a revolt against Governor Victoria, and was subsequently named interim *jefe politico* (governor). However, the *ayuntamiento* (city council) of Los Angeles, refused to recognize him, and he stepped down, saying that he did not wish to defy the peoples' wishes. In 1845, after another revolt removed Governor Micheltorena, Pico was again declared interim governor. This time, the Mexican government, of which Alta California was a territory, confirmed his appointment, and he took the oath of office.

Pico mounted very little resistance to U.S. forces during the Mexican-American War, and foreseeing inevitable defeat, he ultimately fled to Mexico and did not return to Alta California for two years. When he returned, in 1848, he remained a private citizen, serving briefly on the Los Angeles City Council and then as Los Angeles County Assessor. He later built and operated a deluxe hotel in downtown Los Angeles, **Pico House,** which is now a historic monument.

Like many **californios**—Mexican settlers of California—Pico lost all of his considerable land holdings after California became part of the United States, in spite of guarantees in the **Treaty of Guadalupe Hidalgo** that original land grants would be honored. Although he lived a long life, Pico died virtually penniless, at the age of 93.

Juan N. Seguín
(1806–1890)

Born to a wealthy, land-owning family in San Antonio, **Juan Nepomuceno Seguín** became a military leader and a politician who played a key role in the fight for **Texas** independence.

Seguín displayed his leadership abilities at an early age. He entered local politics at 18, and was later elected mayor of the city of San Antonio. During this time, Texas was a part of the Mexican state of Coahuila. The area was experiencing a large influx of Anglos from the United States, who eventually outnumbered the Mexican descendants, or *tejanos*, who lived there.

In 1833, Seguín organized a rally to recruit volunteers to join the army of **Stephen Austin**, who was waging war for Texas independence against the Mexican dictator, President General Antonio López de Santa Anna. Seguín fought at the battle of Concepción with the famous frontiersman Jim Bowie. Afterwards, Austin appointed Seguín captain of the Texas cavalry.

In 1835, Seguín helped Austin defeat the Mexican army in the first **Battle of the Alamo**. The Mexicans came back in 1836, with General Santa Anna himself leading the forces. In the famous battle, Seguín led the tejano contingent of the rebel forces against the Mexican army. Fortunately for Seguín, he was out seeking reinforcements when Santa Anna and his men regained the Alamo, killing all its defenders in the process.

After the Alamo defeat, **Sam Houston**, commander of the rebel Texas forces, promoted Seguín to colonel and made him military commander of San Antonio. Seguín fought with distinction in the **Battle of San Jacinto**, where General Santa Anna was taken prisoner, and after which Texas declared its independence as the Lone Star Republic.

After the war, Seguín returned to San Antonio. He was elected to the Texas senate and in 1840, was reelected mayor of San Antonio. During this time, hostilities between tejanos and Anglos intensified, as Anglos coveted the desirable land that many of the tejanos had owned for generations.

In 1842, after receiving death threats and experiencing other forms of discrimination, Seguín fled Texas for Mexico. However, his military exploits made him a wanted man there. He was taken prisoner at the border and conscripted into the Mexican army, where ironically a few years later he fought against the United States in the Mexican-American War.

Seguín had hoped that Texas would remain an independent republic. However, in 1845, the United States annexed Texas as the 28th state of the Union. Seguín spent part of the remainder of his life in Texas and part of it in Mexico, in the border town of Nuevo Lareda. In 1853, the newly incorporated town of Walnut Springs, Texas renamed itself Seguín, in his honor.

Juan Seguín

Mariano Vallejo

Mariano Guadalupe Vallejo played an important role in the early history of **California** as it passed under the government of three different nations.

Vallejo was born into a wealthy, influential family that was well established in the remote regions of the Mexican state of Alta (Upper) California. He took an interest in public life early when, at the age of ten, he witnessed an attack on his hometown during the Mexican war for independence from Spain.

After Mexico had won its independence, at the age of 15, Vallejo became a military cadet in the Mexican army. He was stationed at the presidio of Monterey. Four years later, he was relocated to the **San Francisco** presidio, and he was elected to the California legislature.

Vallejo saw his first military action when he led a contingency of soldiers to the mission of San Jose to quell an Indian insurrection. A few years later, he was promoted to commander of the San Francisco presidio.

In the 1830s, Vallejo ran the missions at San Francisco Solano and San Rafael Arcangel. He also created Mexican settlements near Fort Ross, north of San Francisco, to counter the growing population of Russian hunters there. In 1833, he was promoted to military chief of the northern half of Alta California, and in 1844, he was elected to the Mexican congress.

About this time, the Mexican government began to secularize the missions. Wealthy men, like Vallejo, bought up much of the land. Eventually, he owned more than 250,000 acres of prime farmland in the area northwest of San Francisco.

In 1836, Californians revolted against Mexican rule, in what became known as the **Bear Flag Rebellion**. Although Vallejo supported United States annexation of California, the Bear Flaggers were Anglos who trusted no one of Mexican descent. They took Vallejo hostage and threw him in prison for two months.

While in prison, Vallejo lost much of his land. He attempted, with little success, to retrieve it after his release. California eventually became a part of the United States and Vallejo continued to participate in civic affairs. He helped draft a state constitution and was one of the first senators elected to the new state legislature in 1850.

In 1851, Vallejo gave land to the state of California on the promise that it would be declared the capital. The city of Vallejo was California's capital from 1852 to 1853. Vallejo retired to his remaining 280 acres of land and took up writing and wine making. He wrote a history of California, and helped develop a fledgling **wine industry** in an area that is now world famous—the **Napa Valley**.

14. Romualdo Pacheco
(1831–1899)

The first Hispanic ever to serve in the United States Congress, **Romualdo Pacheco** was born to a prominent family in **Santa Barbara**, California during the Mexican era. His father, Captain Pacheco, was a native of the Mexican state of Guanajuato who came to California as an aide-de-camp to Governor Echeandia.

When he was 12, Pacheco went to work as an apprentice on a trading vessel. He became an excellent seaman, as well as a skilled horseman and a miner during the **California Gold Rush**.

Pacheco began his political career in 1853 when he was elected judge of the San Luis Obispo Superior Court. California had become a part of the United States, and tensions existed between californios—prominent families who had owned land under the Mexican government—and the newly arrived Anglos. Pacheco was a skilled politician who spoke fluent Spanish and English, and he was able to win the support of both groups.

In 1857, Pacheco won a seat in the **California State Senate** as a member of the Democratic party. Like all other politicians, during this time he became embroiled in the national debate over slavery and the **Civil War**. Pacheco was an abolitionist and a loyal unionist. In the 1860s, he changed his registration to the Republican party.

Pacheco was reelected to the state senate twice in the early 1860s, but each time his service was interrupted. He was appointed brigadier general during the Civil War in 1861, and he was elected state treasurer in 1863.

In 1869, Pacheco was elected to the state senate again, and in 1871, he was elected lieutenant governor. Four years later, he became governor, when the current governor won a seat in the U.S. Senate. Pacheco was the first, and only, Hispanic to serve as California governor since the state joined the union.

In 1876, Pacheco was elected to the **U.S. House of Representatives** by only one vote. The California Supreme Court seated him briefly in the fall of the next year, but his opponent protested, and in 1878 the House Committee on Elections denied Pacheco's certification.

Pacheco was elected to the House again in 1878 and reelected two years later. In addition to becoming the first Hispanic ever to serve in the U.S. Congress, as chairman of the Committee on Private Land Claims, he was the first Hispanic to chair a standing committee.

After serving in Congress, Pacheco was appointed U.S. Envoy Extraordinary and Minister Plenipotentiary to the Central American States. He was responsible for maintaining diplomatic relations with the region. He retired to California in 1893, and died in Oakland six years later.

Romualdo Pacheco

15. Joaquín Murieta
(1832–1853)

Joaquín Murieta migrated from Mexico to the California gold country in 1850, when he was 18 years old. He worked peacefully as a miner until a group of white settlers attacked him and his family. They murdered his brother, assaulted his wife, and beat him brutally. He recovered, but the event transformed him into a Robin Hood-like character, seeking vengeance for all Mexicans who had been mistreated.

With his sidekick, **"Three-Fingers" Jack Garcia**, and their gang of bandits, Murieta began a campaign of robberies targeting white settlers in the gold country. Reports from surviving victims gave rise to a "Joaquin scare." Some believed there were as many as five different Joaquins.

In 1853, the California legislature responded to the panic by forming a special unit of 20 soldiers, led by a former army officer from Texas, **Harry S. Love**, to hunt down Joaquin, whether he was one man or five. Mexican-Americans in the legislature protested the lack of certainty, but the white majority downplayed their concerns. Governor John Bigler posted his own reward of $1,000.

The men searched the foothills of California, and on July 25, with only a few days remaining on the bounty, they encountered a group of Mexican men in an encampment in the Arroyo Cantua, about 70 miles southwest of Fresno. A shoot-out ensued, leaving two men dead: Murieta and "Three-Fingers" Jack.

Poster announcing an exhibit of Joaquín Murieta's head

Love and his men returned to Sacramento with the head of Murieta and the hand of "Three-Fingers" Jack pickled in whiskey jars. Although they could not prove the identity of the victims, the legislature accepted the jars as evidence and rewarded Love with $5,000.

Little is certain about the details of Murieta's life. Some believe he may even have escaped capture in California and returned to Mexico where he died of old age. That Murieta became an icon for Mexican-Americans is indisputable. Soon after the events of 1850, a half-Cherokee journalist named **John Rollin Ridge**, otherwise known as **Yellow Bird**, published a novel entitled, *The Life and Adventures of Joaquín* Murieta, which romanticized his life and fueled the legend.

The story has inspired books, poems, plays, and movies in the United States and abroad. Murieta is believed to have inspired such movie and television characters as Zorro and the Cisco Kid. Murieta was an icon of the Chicano civil rights movement, and **Rodolfo "Corky" Gonzales** (see no. 52) is believed to have based his epic poem, "I Am Joaquín" on Murieta. Every year, a group of more than 200 Mexican-Americans ride horses to Arroyo Cantua on July 25 to pay tribute to the spirit of Murieta and his rebelliousness against oppression and discrimination.

16. Carlos Juan Finlay (1833- 1915) Juan Guiteras (1852–1925)

Two Cuban-born physicians, **Carlos Juan Finlay** and **Juan Guiteras**, endured years of ridicule and skepticism from the medical establishment while they advanced novel theories to explain the spread of **yellow fever.** Eventually, their theories were accepted, and doctors were able to control the deadly disease.

Both men were raised in Cuba and later studied medicine in the United States. As practicing physicians, Finlay and Guiteras also became experts in the study of tropical diseases, such as yellow fever and malaria, for which, at the time, there were no known cures.

Guiteras and Finlay worked together on the **Havana yellow fever commission** in 1879. Guiteras supported Finlay's theory that yellow fever was spread by the bite of the common Havana mosquito, known in scientific terms as the *Aedes aegypti*. Neither doctor could prove the theory, however, and the skeptical medical community gave Finlay the unflattering nickname of "mosquito man."

Guiteras also had proposed a novel theory. He observed that people in areas where yellow fever was common developed lifetime immunity to the disease after experiencing several mild bouts of it during childhood. The theory was significant because, if proven to be true, it would mean that doctors could develop a vaccine for the disease.

It was not until 1898, when the **Spanish-American War** erupted and the United States dispatched troops to occupy Cuba, that yellow fever became a high priority for the American medical community. Prompted by the deaths of its soldiers, the U.S. government established another yellow fever commission, directed by **Walter Reed**, who was a highly regarded surgeon in the U.S. Army.

Finlay convinced Reed and the commission to explore his theory about the role of the common Havana mosquito in the transmis-

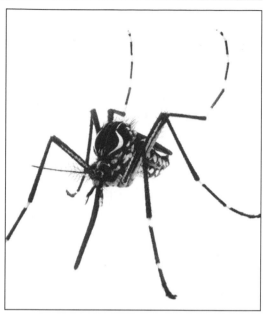

Yellow-fever mosquito

sion of the disease. Finlay and Guiteras worked with the commission and conducted experiments on human volunteers who agreed to be bitten by infected mosquitoes. The Reed commission eventually confirmed the mosquito as the transmitter of yellow fever. After the U.S. government eradicated swamplands in Havana that served as breeding grounds for the insect, the incidence of the disease was dramatically reduced.

Unfortunately, while working with the commission, a number of human volunteers under the supervision of Guiteras died. The outcry over their deaths brought an end to human experimentation. Guiteras was unable to prove his theory and replicate the lifetime immunity that he had observed in adults who had been exposed to yellow fever as children. It was not until 12 years after Guiteras's death, in 1937, that doctors were able to isolate the yellow fever virus and develop a vaccine.

17. Rafael Guastavino
(1842–1908)

Rafael Guastavino brought an ancient Spanish building technique with him to the United States, and used it to design a series of stunning edifices that remain lasting monuments to his architectural genius.

Guastavino was born in Valencia, Spain. He became an **architect** and went to work in Barcelona, where he revived an ancient technique that had been used in the region of Catalonia, where the city is located. The *boveda catalana*, or **Catalan vault**, had been employed and refined centuries earlier by the architects of the region. The method involves using layers of thin clay tiles embedded in mortar to create curved surfaces that result in magnificent vaults or domes.

Guastavino became a successful architect in Spain using this method. He designed large industrial and residential buildings for the wealthy industrialists of Catalonia. He refined the system and moved to America in 1881. However, he did not find immediate success in the United States. He worked only occasionally designing buildings until 1888, when he got his big break.

Aware of his expertise in the vaulting system, an architectural firm hired him to produce the vaulting for the **Boston Public Library**. Although some in the field doubted that a vault could be constructed in such a large space, Guastavino proved them wrong. The success of the building and the vaults that he created brought him immediate recognition. He established the **Guastavino Fireproof Construction Company** in 1889, and it was quickly besieged with requests for work.

The system that Guastavino perfected had several advantages. The vaults spanned large distances with much less weight than the other materials that were commonly used, such as timber or iron beams. Unlike timber, the tiles and mortar were also fireproof. They were also easier to transport and to use in construction on site.

The vaults were visually stunning. Guastavino constructed spectacular buildings throughout the eastern United States, where his work became extremely popular. Some of his most memorable assignments were the Oyster Bar in **Grand Central Station**, the main hall at **Ellis Island**, and the **Cathedral of St. John the Divine**, all of which were in New York City. His work also appeared in buildings in Washington, D.C., and Asheville, North Carolina.

When Guastavino died in 1908, his son took over the company. The Guastavino Fireproof Construction Company survived until the early 1960s. By that time, the dramatic vaulting style, and its expensive labor costs, had fallen out of favor with the modern movement in architecture. However, in the late 1990s, New York City commenced a major project to restore and publicize many of Guastavino's historic works.

Ellis Island

18. Lola Rodriquez de Tió
(1843–1924)

Lola Rodriquez de Tió was born and educated in **Puerto Rico**. Her strong political beliefs, and her lifelong love affair with her native land, inspired her to write several highly acclaimed books of poetry. Through her writing and her political activities, she became an influential player in the Puerto Rican and Cuban **independence movements**, even while she spent much of her adult life in exile.

Born in San Germán, Lola Rodriquez studied in Catholic schools and with private tutors. She was drawn to poetry as a young girl, and she studied with the renowned poet **Ursula Cardona de Quiñones**.

In 1865, Rodriquez married the journalist and political activist, **Bonocio Tió**, and changed her name to Rodriguez de Tió. The newlyweds shared a passion for Puerto Rican independence. The island was then a part of the Spanish colonial empire. Together, they conducted political meetings for members of the literary community at their home in the city of Mayagüez, which helped to ignite an independence movement on the island.

In 1868, Rodriquez de Tió wrote the nationalist lyrics for the hymn "La Borinqueña." The song became the **Puerto Rican national hymn**. In 1876, she published *Mis Cantares* (*My Songs*), her first book of poetry. At the same time, her reputation as an agitator in the independence movement grew, and in 1877, the government exiled her. She and her family were forced to move to Venezuela.

However, the bond to her homeland was too great for Rodriquez de Tió to overcome, and she returned to Puerto Rico three years later. She continued her political activities and her writing there. In 1885, she published her second book of poetry, *Claros y Nieblas* (*Clarities and Cloudiness*). In 1889, she was exiled again. This time, she moved to Cuba.

Lola Rodriquez de Tió

Rodriquez de Tió remained in Cuba and continued her revolutionary activities. She published her third and final book of poetry, *Mi Libro de Cuba* (*My Cuban Book*), in 1893. Two years later, the Cuban government exiled her, and she moved to New York City.

Rodriquez de Tió continued to conspire with leaders of the Puerto Rican and Cuban independence movements while she lived in New York. In 1899, Puerto Rico and Cuba were both liberated from Spanish colonial rule when the United States defeated Spain in the Spanish-American War.

Rodriquez de Tió returned to Cuba, where she received a hero's welcome. She remained there and applied her political energy to a growing **women's liberation** movement. In 1910, she was elected to the Cuban Academy of Arts and Letters. She died in 1924.

19. George Santayana
(1863–1952)

Born in Madrid, Spain, **Jorge Agustín Nicolás Ruiz de Santayana y Borrás** came to the United States as a boy. He moved to Boston in 1872 at the age of nine to live with his mother and his half-brothers and half-sisters.

Santayana changed his name to George, but he still had difficulty acclimating to a new country. In school, the other students bullied him, and he turned to books. At the age of 17, while a student at the Boston Latin School, Santayana won first prize for his poem "Day and Night." He entered **Harvard University** two years later, as a philosophy major, with aspirations of becoming a poet.

After he graduated summa cum laude from Harvard in 1886, Santayana began his graduate studies in philosophy at the University of Berlin, in Germany. He spent some time at Cambridge University, in England, and in 1888, returned to the United States. Three years later, he became the first Hispanic philosopher to receive a Ph.D. from Harvard.

Santayana then took a teaching job at Harvard, but he was not a philosopher's philosopher. He continued to publish poetry, even though the administration pressured him to concentrate on philosophy.

In the mid-1890s, Santayana found a solution. He created a philosophy course in **aesthetics,** which is the study of all things beautiful and artistic. The course allowed Santayana to pursue his interests in literature and poetry in a philosophical context. It became immensely popular.

In 1896, Santayana published his first philosophical work, *The Sense of Beauty*, which included his lectures on aesthetics. The book was highly praised and won the approval of the Harvard administration.

Santayana had found his niche in philosophy. In 1900, he published *Interpretations of Poetry and Religion*, and in 1905-06, he published *The Life of Reason*, a five-volume set, which laid the groundwork for his future ideas.

The book also brought him new fame at Harvard. He was promoted to full professor in 1907, but he was never happy with academics. Santayana retired from teaching in 1912 and spent the remainder of his life traveling and living in Europe.

During this time, Santayana enjoyed the fame and stature of a philosopher renowned worldwide. In the spirit of the detached thinker, for which he became so well known, he published numerous books that reflected his critical thoughts on society and religion.

In 1927, Santayana became the first Hispanic to receive the Gold Medal from the Royal Society of Literature in London. In 1944, he published his autobiography, *Persons and Places*. Santayana died in 1952.

George Santayana

A feminist and poet, **Sara Estela Ramírez** became involved in a number of political causes at the turn of the 20th century. She was ahead of her time, and she made an indelible impression on the politics and culture of **Texas** in her short life.

Ramírez was born in Progreso, Coahuila, Mexico. Her mother died when she was a young girl, and she educated herself and raised her siblings at the same time. She studied to become a teacher and, in 1898, she began her first job, in Laredo, Texas, at the Seminario de Laredo.

In Texas, Ramírez became a **political activist**. While the former Mexican state had been annexed to the United States more than 50 years earlier, tension between Mexicans and Anglos remained high. Discrimination against Hispanics was commonplace. Ramírez became involved with the **Partido Liberal Mexicano** (PLM), an organization that fought for the rights of Mexicans and Mexican-Americans living in Texas.

At that time in Texas, men who spoke out on behalf of the PLM were often harassed and discriminated against. Women activists, however, often were not treated as badly. Being a female activist worked to Ramírez's advantage, and she became one of the most important figures in the PLM.

Ramírez was an outspoken advocate, who wrote poems, essays, and articles and gave speeches that carried the party's message. Her writings and speeches were published in local papers, such as *La Crónica* and *El Demócratica Fronterizo*, and beginning in 1904, she published her own daily periodicals, *La Corregidora* and then *Aurora*. She also wrote and starred in a play which was produced in Laredo playhouses.

Through her involvement with the PLM, Ramírez also became an inspiration to the **labor** and **women's rights movements**. She

La Crónica **newspaper**

gave one of her most famous speeches, "Alocución," at the 24th anniversary of the founding of the *Sociedad de Obreros* (Society of Workers). In it, she described workers as "the arm, the heart of the world. . . integral parts of human progress."

As a feminist before feminism had become a national movement, Ramírez was ahead of her time. Shortly before her death, she wrote one of her most well-known poems, "*A la mujer*" ("To the woman"). In it, she tells women to "rise to life, to activity, to the beauty of really living."

Ramírez enjoyed wide popularity and was a woman of great potential, but unfortunately, her life ended early. She died in 1910, at the age of 29, of an unidentified illness.

Ignacio E. Lozano

When **Ignacio Lozano** brought his family to the United States, he could not have envisioned the impact he would have on the culture of his adopted country.

The only son of six children, Lozano learned responsibility at an early age; when he was still a youth, his father died, leaving him the only man in the family. In 1910, seeking to escape the escalating turmoil of the Mexican Revolution, Lozano took his mother and five sisters across the border to **San Antonio**, Texas, which became his permanent home.

Lozano was always interested in journalism, and to help support his family, he began taking odd jobs at Spanish language newspapers. In 1913, he left his job and started his own weekly **Spanish language newspaper,** called *La Prensa*. The paper was so successful that he converted it to a daily after just one year.

Eventually, readers in the Hispanic communities of other U.S. cities began to take notice. In particular, *La Prensa* developed a popular following among the growing Hispanic community of **Los Angeles**. Lozano saw an opportunity there, so in 1926, on September 16, Mexican Independence Day, he started a second paper—*La Opinión*.

Lozano remained in San Antonio where he worked full-time on *La Prensa*, but he visited Los Angeles frequently to tend to the business of *La Opinión*. Eventually, he sent his young son, **Ignacio Jr.**, to Los Angeles to run *La Opinión* as its assistant publisher.

For a long time, *La Prensa* was still the bigger, more successful paper. However, with the ever larger number of Hispanics living in the Los Angeles area, *La Opinión* gradually gained in popularity. During the 1940s, it had a circulation of around 12,000. By 1953, *La Opinión* had eclipsed *La Prensa* in circulation and profits.

Although Lozano remained in the United States, he never lost his interest in the affairs of Mexico. Both of his newspapers reflected this emphasis. Their stories focused primarily on Mexican issues, as opposed to U.S. issues.

In the 1950s, the Lozano family sold *La Prensa* and concentrated its efforts on *La Opinión*. Eventually, *La Prensa* went out of business. Ignacio Lozano died in 1953, at which time Ignacio Jr. took over as publisher. Unlike his father, the younger Lozano was an American citizen and a resident of Los Angeles, and he shifted the emphasis of *La Opinión* from a "Mexican paper in Los Angeles to an American paper in the Spanish language."

Ignacio Jr. retired in 1986, but the Lozano family retained ownership of *La Opinión*. At the start of the 21st century, it was the most widely read Spanish-language newspaper in the United States, with more 500,000 readers. It celebrated its 75th anniversary in September 2001.

22. Lucrezia Bori
(1887–1960)

Born in Valencia, Spain, **Lucrecia Borja y González de Riancho** rose to fame as the beloved grand dame of New York's **Metropolitan Opera** in the early 1900s. She adopted "Bori" as her stage name.

She made her first singing performance at the age of six, when she appeared in a benefit concert in her hometown. At the age of 16, she traveled to Milan, Italy to receive voice training.

Recognized quickly as a talented performer, Bori was hired by the Italian opera house, **La Scala**, a year after she moved to Italy. Eventually she joined the touring New York Metropolitan Opera in Paris, and in 1910, performed her first role, when she replaced a sick colleague.

Lucrezia Bori

Bori portrayed the role of Manon, in Puccini's famous opera, *Manon Lescaut,* performing opposite the legendary Italian tenor **Enrico Caruso**. The performance sold out, she was an immediate sensation, and two more performances were quickly scheduled.

In 1911, her singing caught the attention of German composer **Richard Strauss**, who insisted that she perform the role of Octavian in the local premiere of his opera *Der Rosenkavalier.*

In 1912, at the age of 24, Bori performed her Manon role at the opening night for the Met in New York, her first appearance in the United States. She continued to star for the Met until 1915, when she underwent throat surgery.

Bori spent five years of lonely convalescence recovering from her surgery. She could not sing, or even speak, for months. Finally, in 1921, she returned to the Met, where she starred for another 15 years.

Throughout her career, Bori wowed audiences with her clear voice and passion. She exuded charm and vulnerability. She starred in a number of memorable roles, including Mimi in *La Bohème,* Norina in *Don Pasquale,* Juliette in *Roméo et Juliette,* and Violetta in *La traviata.* In all, she starred in 29 roles, in more than 600 performances, over 19 seasons with the Metropolitan Opera.

In 1936, Bori gave her final performance. She was still at the peak of her talent, and the audience gave her a 20-minute standing ovation.

Although she retired from singing, Bori did not leave the Met. The country was in the midst of the Great Depression, but she drew on her tremendous popularity and star quality to help raise funds for the opera. Her efforts earned her the nickname "**the opera's Joan of Arc.**" Building on her success as a fund-raiser, Bori became the first active artist, and the first woman, elected to the Met's Board of Directors. She was elected president of the Metropolitan Opera Guild in 1942.

23. Dennis Chavez
(1888–1962)

The lone voice for Hispanic-Americans in the national political arena for decades, **Dionisio Chavez** knew all about overcoming obstacles. The third child of eight, he was born in the town of Los Chavez in the United States Mexican territory that later became the state of **New Mexico**.

When he was seven, Chavez's family moved to Albuquerque and changed his given name to Dennis. Although he was an enthusiastic student, Chavez quit school in the eighth grade and took a job driving a grocery delivery wagon to help support the family.

Dennis Chavez

Even though he'd left school, Chavez continued to learn. He studied surveying, and in 1905 qualified for a job with the Albuquerque Engineering Department. He also continued to visit the library at night, reading up on politics and Thomas Jefferson, his two favorite subjects.

Chavez failed in his first attempt at public office, a run for county clerk. In 1916, he took a job as an interpreter for U.S. Senate candidate **Andrieus A. Jones**. Jones won his election and offered Chavez a job as a senate clerk. Chavez took the job, and he entered Georgetown University in Washington, D.C. by passing a special entrance exam taken in lieu of a high school diploma.

In 1920, Chavez earned his bachelor of law degree from Georgetown. Then he returned to Albuquerque to open a law practice. He became active in local politics, and was elected to the **New Mexico House of Representatives**. In 1930, Chavez ran for New Mexico's lone seat in the **U.S. Congress**. He defeated the incumbent and was reelected two years later.

After two terms, Chavez set his sights on the **U.S. Senate**. In 1934, he ran against another incumbent, Senator Bronson Cutting, and lost by a narrow margin One year later, Cutting was killed in a plane crash, and Chavez was appointed by the governor to replace him. Chavez was officially elected to retain the seat a year later. The voters reelected him five more times during his career, which lasted more than 30 years.

Throughout his tenure in the Senate, Chavez was a dedicated liberal and a tireless defender of Mexican-Americans, Native Americans, farmers, and labor. For much of the time, he was the lone voice representing Mexican-Americans in the national halls of government. He was frequently controversial and always independent.

Chavez is best known for his relentless crusade to create a federal **Fair Employment Practices Commission**, which would guarantee employees of government-contracted companies that they could not be discriminated against because of their race, creed, color, or sex. Chavez did not succeed in passing such a bill during his lifetime, but the commission was eventually created in the 1960s.

Maria Latigo Hernandez fought for the rights of Hispanic-Americans for more than 60 years, as an activist, author, and radio and television host.

Born in Mexico, Hernandez came to the United States as a young girl when her family fled the turmoil of the Mexican Revolution. They settled in Texas, and in 1915, she married Pedro Hernandez. Several years later, after settling in San Antonio, the couple joined a civic-oriented group known as **La Orden Hijos de America** (The Order of the Children of America). It was the beginning of a lifelong partnership in community activism.

In the early 1920s, Hernandez trained as a midwife and spent several years giving medical care to the poor. During that time, she remained involved in civil rights issues. She advocated for women's rights, wrote articles, gave speeches only in Spanish, and emphasized Hispanic cultural awareness. Because of this, she clashed with other fledgling civil rights groups, such as the **League of United Latin American Citizens** (LULAC), which disregarded feminist issues and emphasized assimilation as a strategy to improve the lives of Hispanic-Americans.

In 1929, Hernandez and her husband founded their own civil rights group, **Orden Caballeros de America** (the Order of the Knights of America), which became a vehicle for their lifelong activism. In 1934, she founded **La Liga Por Defensa Escolar en San Antonio** (the Scholastic Defense League of San Antonio), which utilized rallies and marches to call attention to the deplorable conditions of local schools for Mexican-American children.

Hernandez was an outstanding orator, and in the 1930s, she hosted one of the first Spanish-speaking radio programs in San Antonio, "La Voz de las Americas" ("The Voice of the Americas"). In the 1960s, she hosted a weekly television program called "La Hora de la Mujer" ("The Hour of the Woman").

In 1945, Hernandez wrote a book in which she explained her belief that political activism is a moral and social imperative. She expounded on her philosophies about the role of family and the responsibilities of community leaders.

Mexican-American school

Hernandez and her husband remained active even after they had reached retirement age. During the 1960s and '70s, they became active in the Chicano movement, especially with the **La Raza Unida Party** (LRUP), which formed in Texas in 1970 to increase Mexican-American voter registration and political power. In 1970, she was the keynote speaker at the LRUP's statewide conference, and in 1972, she and her husband traveled throughout Texas campaigning for the party's candidates for statewide office.

In spite of her dedication, Hernandez still had time for family life. When she died in 1986, she was survived by 5 children, 19 grandchildren, 23 great-grandchildren, and 8 great-great-grandchildren.

25. Carlos Castaneda
(1896–1958)

Carlos Castaneda was a noted **historian** who specialized in the history of Mexico and the Southwestern United States. His work emphasized the common history of Mexicans and Americans in the state of Texas.

Castaneda was born, the seventh of eight children, in Ciudad Camargo on the Rio Grande River in the Mexican border state of Tamaulipas. When Castaneda was 12 years old, the family fled to Brownsville, Texas to escape the Mexican Revolution. Two years later, both parents died within months of each other.

In spite of his hardships, Castaneda excelled early in school. He enrolled in summer school to improve his English skills, and he graduated as the valedictorian of Brownsville High School in 1916, the only Mexican-American in his class.

Castaneda earned an academic scholarship to the **University of Texas at Austin**, where he enrolled as an engineering student. He later switched his major to history. After two interruptions, one to serve as a machine gun instructor in World War I and another caused by lack of money, he graduated, Phi Beta Kappa, in 1921.

After college, Castaneda worked as a high school teacher in San Antonio and studied for his master's degree in history. He earned his M.A. in 1923 and took a job as an associate professor of modern languages at the **College of William and Mary** in Virginia, where he taught Spanish for four years. In 1927, he returned to the University of Texas at Austin to head the **Latin American Collection** of the university library.

In 1928, Castaneda published *The Mexican Side of the Texas Revolution*, which documented the events of 1836, based on translations of Mexican eyewitness accounts. Four years later, in 1932, he completed his Ph.D. dissertation, a critical translation of "Fray Juan Agustin Morfi's History of Texas: 1673-1779." The dissertation was so well received that it was published three years later.

The recognition he gained from his dissertation helped earn Castaneda a commission from the Texas Historical Commission of the Knights of Columbus to write a history of the Catholic Church in Texas for the 1936 state centennial. He expanded on the theme, which over the course of 14 years became his seminal seven-volume work, *Our Catholic Heritage in Texas, 1519-1936*.

In 1939, Castaneda joined the University of Texas History Department as a part-time faculty member. He became a full professor in 1946. In the 1940s, he was also appointed special assistant to the federal government's **Fair Employment Practices Committee** (FEPC). The FEPC monitored companies' hiring practices to make sure they did not discriminate against nonwhites. His work was instrumental in improving racial equality in the Texas oil industry.

Carlos Castenada

26. Xavier Cugat
(1900–1990)

Francisco De Asis Javier Cugat Mingall De Cru Y Deulofeo was born in Gerona, Spain. He immigrated with his family to Cuba in 1905.

When he was a young boy in Havana, Cugat received a miniature fiddle from a neighbor who was a violin maker. He studied classical violin and soon became an expert. By the time he was eight, he was performing in cafés, and at the age of 12, he was first violin with the orchestra of the **Teatro Nacional in Havana.**

Cugat became a solo violinist and immigrated to the United States when he was in his early twenties. He continued to study and perform there, and he traveled the world with the renowned opera tenor **Enrico Caruso.** Cugat also played occasionally in dance bands. However, success was elusive, and there were times when he found himself sleeping on a bench in Central Park in New York City. Unable to make a living as a solo violinist, Cugat moved to California, and utilizing one of his other talents, he took a job as a cartoonist for the *Los Angeles Times.*

However, Cugat couldn't stay away from music for long. After a few years, he took it up again. This time he took a different approach, focusing instead on dance music. In 1928, he formed a dance orchestra, the **Latin American Band**, which played regularly at the famous **Coconut Grove** in Los Angeles. The Latin American Band later became the house band for the **Waldorf Astoria** hotel in New York City, where they performed for 16 years.

During the 1930s, Cugat and his band led the nation in an Afro-Cuban music craze. Cugat had a talent for arranging music with unique and exotic Caribbean rhythms that

Xavier Cugat with Linda Romay

appealed to American tastes. The band was instrumental in popularizing dances such as the rumba, the tango, and the mambo.

Cugat was criticized for his commercialism, but he was not shy about his desire to succeed as a musician. He once said, "I would rather play "Chiquita Banana" and have my swimming pool than play Bach and starve." He is also credited with inventing a unique percussion instrument, the **congat**, which is a cross between the bongo and conga drums.

Cugat appeared as himself in a number of movies in the 1930s and '40s. His credits include *Go West Young Man*, *You Were Never Lovelier*, and *Holiday in Mexico.* Cugat's band always featured beautiful young singing stars, a number of whom he married. His wives included the well-known singers Rita Montaner, Carmen Castillo, Lorraine Allen, Abbe Lane, and Charo.

Cugat retired in 1970 and moved to Barcelona, Spain, where he died in 1990.

27. Severo Ochoa
(1905–1993)

Nobel-prize winning **biochemist Severo Ochoa** spent his life studying the basic chemistry of living organisms. His research revolutionized the science of **genetics** and aided the search for a cure for cancer.

Born in the small fishing town of Luarca in northern Spain, Ochoa received his B.A. from Malaga College in 1921. He earned his medical degree from the University of Madrid in 1929; however, he never became a practicing physician. Instead, he pursued the study of organic chemistry, which was his passion.

Before he finished his medical studies, Ochoa worked as a research assistant in physiology at the University of Glasgow in Scotland. After he received his degree, he spent two years in Germany, at the Kaiser Wilhelm Institute for Biology and the University of Heidelberg's Institute for Medical Research. In 1931, he returned to the University of Madrid School of Medicine as a lecturer and head of the physiology department. In the late 1930s, he taught and did research for two years at the Oxford University Medical School in England.

Severo Ochoa

In 1940, after the end of the Spanish Civil War and the rise to power of General **Francisco Franco** and the Falange (Fascist) Party, Ochoa decided not to return to Spain. Instead, he moved to the United States, and he eventually became an American citizen in 1956.

In the United States, Ochoa first worked as a lecturer and researcher at the medical school of Washington University in St. Louis. He later conducted research at the New York University Bellevue Medical Center.

While in New York, Ochoa continued the research on **enzymes** he had begun in Europe. He advanced theories that these chemicals in plant and animal tissue allow living organisms to convert food into energy, in the process known as **metabolism**. Later, he applied his research in this field to the study of DNA, which is the genetic code for all living organisms. He announced a discovery about the basic chemicals that allow cells to produce nucleic acids, or **protein**.

Ochoa's discoveries helped scientists understand how certain diseases are spread, especially cancer, which involves abnormal cell reproduction. His findings also advanced the field of genetic engineering, which was then in its infancy.

For their work in this field, Ochoa and his colleague, Dr. **Arthur Kornberg**, were awarded the Nobel Prize in physiology or medicine in 1959. It was one of many honors Ochoa received throughout his career.

After the death of his wife, Carmen, Ochoa returned to Spain in 1985. He died there in 1993.

28. José Arcadia Limón
(1908–1972)

One of America's premiere **modern dancers** and **choreographers**, **José Arcadia Limón** originally thought he wanted to become a painter.

He was born in Culiaca, Sinaloa, Mexico. His father was the director of the State Music Academy and traveled the country with the national military band. During the Mexican Revolution, the family moved to the border town of Nogales. Later, they settled in Tucson, Arizona.

The family relocated to Los Angeles, where Limón attended high school. As a student, he was active in the arts and dreamed of becoming an artist. After high school, he enrolled at the University of California, but he dropped out after his mother died. He went to work in a factory to help support his large family.

Limón had developed a circle of artist friends, and in 1928, he followed them to New York City. He had saved up $27, and he hitchhiked across the country for ten days to get there. He enrolled in art school, but after six months, he realized that he did not want to become a painter after all.

The next year, Limón attended a performance by a modern dancer from Germany at the **Knickerbocker Theater.** The performance was transforming—Limón realized that this was what he wanted to do with the rest of his life. He began to study modern dance with the masters, and in three years, he was performing on Broadway. In 1932, he made his first appearance in the **Humphrey-Weidman Company** production of the play *Americana*.

While he was performing with Humphrey-Weidman, Limón met a young receptionist named Pauline, who would later become his wife and business manager of 30 years.

During the 1930s, Limón also taught modern dance at Bennington College in Vermont, and he began composing his own dance productions. In 1937, he choreographed his first group dance, *Danza de la Muerte* (Dance of Death).

Limón served in the U.S. army for three years during World War II. After he finished his military service in 1945, he formed a small dance company. In 1949, he produced his own original work, *The Moor's Pavane*, based on Shakespeare's play Othello. It is considered one of his greatest productions. His work was unique in its expression of his personal vision, critique of social injustices, and incorporation of Mexican themes.

Limón taught modern dance at universities throughout the United States, and he traveled around the globe, performing and teaching in Europe, Mexico, and South America. He continued to dance and choreograph until his death. Some of his last productions were performed only a month before he died.

José Arcadia Limón

Carmen Miranda

Maria do Carmo Miranda da Cunha, "The Brazilian Bombshell," was born in the small town of Marco de Canavezes, near Lisbon, Portugal. Her family moved to the Brazilian city of Rio de Janeiro when she was a baby.

Miranda was raised in a convent school and later worked as a hat maker and a model in a Rio department store. When a musician discovered her singing on the job there, he was so impressed that he got her work on a radio show. Soon, she was performing in Brazilian nightclubs and movies; when an American theatrical producer saw her nightclub act, he invited her to come to New York to perform on **Broadway**.

In 1939, Miranda appeared in the Broadway musical, *The Streets of Paris*, and immediately became a star in the United States. She followed up with an appearance in a nightclub act at the Waldorf Astoria hotel and later moved to **Hollywood**.

Miranda appeared in a string of movies in the early 1940s, such as *Down Argentine Way* and *Week-End in Havana*. Her most memorable performance came in the 1943 movie entitled *The Gang's All Here*, in which she performed "**The Lady in the Tutti-Frutti Hat**," a song that was created especially for her.

The song was apropos for the character that Miranda had created. All of her movies revolved around exotic, tropical locales, and for the films, Miranda developed a comic female character that combined a mix of exaggerated Hispanic stereotypes. For her roles, she wore elaborate costumes that included platform shoes and oversized hats filled with fruit.

Miranda's career in the United States was short-lived. She had reached her peak during a time when interest in Latin America was high. President Franklin D. Roosevelt had implemented the **Good Neighbor Policy** designed to court friendships with Latin American countries in order to fend off fascism in the region. However, after World War II, America's political focus shifted to the Soviet Union and the spread of communism in Eastern Europe. Interest in Latin America waned, and so did Miranda's career. She made only a few movies in the late 1940s, and in 1955, she died of a heart attack, at the age of 46, after appearing on a television show with the comedian Jimmy Durante.

Even after her death, Miranda inspired the creation of another character, the woman who appeared in television commercials for Chiquita Banana. The woman wore a headdress made of bananas and sang a song about the product. However, audiences by this time were sensitive to the offensive nature of the character, and the ads were eventually dropped.

30. Luis Alvarez
(1911–1988)

Luis Alvarez was a Nobel Prize-winning **physicist** whose work had a profound effect on the course of science and history in the 20th century.

Alvarez was born in 1911 in San Francisco, California, where his father was a well-known physician and medical researcher at the University of California Medical School. His father later moved the family to Rochester, Minnesota, so he could work at the world-renowned Mayo Clinic.

As a young student, Alvarez excelled in the sciences. He began to show an interest in physics, and his father hired a colleague to tutor him. The training paid off. Alvarez enrolled at the University of Chicago in 1928 and received his bachelor's degree in physics in 1932; four years later, he received his Ph.D.

After he received his doctorate, Alvarez returned to California to join the faculty of the **University of California at Berkeley** as a research scientist. He remained affiliated with UC Berkeley until he retired from academics in 1978.

At Berkeley, Alvarez began to study atomic energy and structure. Later, he conducted important military research at the **Massachusetts Institute of Technology**, immediately prior to the entry of the United States into World War II. While at M.I.T, he collaborated with other scientists to develop the first **radar systems**. He developed a bombing targeting system, a microwave early warning system, and a narrow beam radar system to enable planes to land in bad weather.

When the United States became involved in the war, Alvarez was assigned to the **Manhattan Project** at the Los Alamos Laboratory in New Mexico. Here scientists developed the detonating device that was used for the first **atomic bombs,** two of which were dropped on the Japanese cities of Hiroshima and Nagasaki. Alvarez came to terms with his involvement in the project, saying that it helped bring about a swift end to the war and prevented the loss of more lives.

Luis Alvarez

After the war, Alvarez returned to UC Berkeley as a professor, refining and developing new instruments for the study of **sub-atomic particles**. He discovered dozens of new elementary particles, and his work paved the way for new research and discoveries in high energy physics. He received the ultimate recognition for his work in 1968, when he was awarded the Nobel Prize in physics.

Alvarez continued to explore new fields of science even after he became a Nobel laureate. Based on his discovery of a rare mineral element on a trip to Italy, he developed a theory about a giant meteor that crashed to earth 65 million years ago. He theorized that the collision formed a dust cloud, which obscured the sun, bringing about the extinction of the dinosaurs. The theory is still the subject of debate in scientific circles.

The events of Dr. **Hector Perez Garcia's** early life helped shape his attitude towards race relations in the United States. Born in the town of Liera, Mexico in 1914, Garcia came to America as a boy, during the Mexican Revolution, when his parents immigrated to Mercedes, Texas after escaping an attack on their village.

In Mexico, Garcia's father was a college professor and his mother was a school teacher, but the family worked in the fields in Texas to survive. His parents emphasized education as the best tool to overcome discrimination. When one of his teachers proclaimed, "No Mexican will ever make an 'A' in my class," Garcia considered it a challenge and followed his parents' advice. He graduated as the valedictorian of his high school class and earned his B.A. in zoology with honors from the University of Texas in 1936.

After earning his degree, Garcia applied to the University of Texas Medical School, during an era of strictly enforced quotas. With his exceptional academic record, he beat out the competition for one spot allotted to Mexican-Americans and went on to earn his medical degree in 1940.

Garcia volunteered for army duty the following year. He served as an infantry officer, a combat engineer officer, and a medical corps officer during World War II. He served in North Africa and Italy, earning a Bronze Star and six Battle Stars before being honorably discharged as a major.

After the war, Garcia opened a medical practice in Corpus Christi, Texas. With his office located near the U.S. Veterans Administration building, he tended to many Hispanic veterans who were denied treatment by military hospitals.

Responding to the injustice, Garcia formed the **American GI Forum** to guarantee Mexican-American veterans the health and educational benefits to which they were entitled. Shortly thereafter, the organization and Dr. Garcia responded to an outrageous act of discrimination in the town of Three Rivers, Texas.

Local cemetery officials refused to bury the body of one of the town's soldiers because he was Hispanic. Private **Felix Longoria** had been killed in action in the Philippines. Through the advocacy of the Forum and Dr. Garcia, and the help of Lyndon Johnson, then a Texas U.S. Senator, Private Longoria eventually received burial with full military honors in Arlington National Cemetery.

Under Garcia's leadership, the American GI Forum grew into one of the largest and most effective national civil rights organizations in the country. Garcia continued to advocate for Hispanic issues throughout his life. He became involved in national politics, was appointed by President Lyndon Johnson to the **U.S. Commission on Civil Rights** and, in 1984, was awarded the **Presidential Medal of Freedom**.

Hector Garcia

32. Anthony Quinn
(1915–2001)

Known worldwide as Zorba, from the hit film *Zorba the Greek*, **Anthony Quinn** won numerous honors for a variety of stage and film roles in a career that spanned more than six decades.

Anthony Rudolph Oaxaca Quinn was born in the Mexican state of Chihuahua. When he was a baby, his father left home to fight in the Mexican Revolution, and his mother smuggled the family across the border to El Paso, Texas. His father reunited with the family in Los Angeles. At the age of nine, Quinn was forced to take odd jobs to help support the family after his father died in a car accident.

In school, Quinn was a gifted student in a variety of subjects. He wanted to take acting classes, but he was unable to perform in school plays because of a speech impediment. He had the defect surgically corrected when he was 18.

In the 1930s, Quinn got his first professional acting assignments. After he won the part of an Indian in Cecil B. DeMille's western movie *The Plainsman*, he went under contract with Paramount Studios and appeared in a number of films during the 1940s.

Because he was getting only minor roles, mostly as villains of various stereotyped ethnicities and nationalities, Mexican and otherwise, Quinn became dissatisfied with Hollywood. In 1947, he entered a career in theater. Most notably, he performed the lead in a production of *A Streetcar Named Desire*, which had a successful two-year run.

Quinn eventually returned to Hollywood and resumed a film career. He won an **Academy Award** for supporting actor for his role as the brother to Mexican revolutionary, Emiliano Zapata, in the 1952 film *Viva Zapata!* In 1956, he took home another supporting actor Oscar for the role of the artist Paul Gaugin, in the film *Lust for Life*.

In spite of his two Oscars, Quinn was still dissatisfied with Hollywood, and he returned to the stage once again. However, during the 1960s, he went back to movies and gave his most famous performance, as the Greek peasant Zorba, in the film *Zorba the Greek*. The film was an international hit that was nominated for several Oscars, including best actor for Quinn.

Anthony Quinn

Throughout his career, the handsome and flamboyant Quinn had a reputation for being a ladies' man, and was involved in numerous romantic affairs. He married twice, and fathered eleven children, the last of which was born when he was 78 years old.

Quinn made more than 325 films during his career. He acted into his eighties, appearing in the film *A Walk in the Clouds* in 1995.

One of the most outspoken members to serve in Congress, **Enrique Barbosa Gonzáles**, was born in San Antonio, Texas. His father had been the mayor of the town of Mapimi in the Mexican state of Durango, but in 1911, the family fled to Texas to escape the Mexican Revolution.

Gonzáles was raised in San Antonio, where he attended high school and college. In 1943, he graduated from St. Mary's University School of Law. After law school, he worked for military and naval intelligence as a cable and radio censor during World War II.

In the 1950s, Gonzáles embarked on a career in politics. He was elected to the San Antonio City Council in 1953, and he served as mayor pro-tempore for part of his first term. While on the city council, Gonzáles began to define himself as an outspoken defender of liberal causes. He denounced segregation of public facilities and helped the city adopt desegregation ordinances.

Henry B. Gonzáles

In 1956, Gonzáles was elected to the **Texas State Senate**. In 1957, he and another legislator filibustered for 36 hours against several segregation bills. It was the longest filibuster in the history of the Texas legislature, and it drew national media attention.

In 1958, Gonzáles made an unsuccessful run for governor of Texas. Two years later, he and U.S. Senator **Dennis Chavez** (see no. 23) of New Mexico served as national co-chairmen of the Viva Kennedy Clubs, which organized Hispanic voters for John F. Kennedy's presidential campaign.

In 1961, Gonzáles became the first Hispanic elected to the **U.S. House of Representatives** from Texas. In the House, he continued his reputation as a crusader. In 1963, he opposed increased funding for the House Committee on Un-American Activities, the controversial committee that had waged an uncompromising campaign against communism. In 1977, he was appointed Chair of the House Assassinations Committee, which was established to investigate the murders of John F. Kennedy and Martin Luther King Jr.; however, he quit his post to protest what he believed was the corrupting influence of organized crime on the investigation.

Gonzáles never ran for office on a Hispanic platform, although many of the causes he championed as a legislator benefited his Hispanic constituents. In the 1960s, he led the charge to end the **bracero program**, which had fostered abusive conditions for nonresident farmworkers, most of whom came from Mexico. During his tenure, he also successfully advocated for civil rights, affordable housing, and small business legislation. As his career progressed, Gonzáles became the elder statesman of Hispanic representatives, having served longer than any other Hispanic in Congress.

Emma Tenayuca
(1916–1999)

Emma Tenayuca was a dedicated activist for the cause of exploited workers in the state of Texas. She was born in San Antonio to interracial parents; her mother was a descendant of Spanish colonialists, and her father was of Indian descent from southern Texas.

At the age of 16, Tenayuca led Mexican female workers on a strike at the **Finck Cigar Company.** Her role landed her in jail, but the publicity brought notoriety to her and the strikers. Shortly after the strike, Tenayuca helped form a chapter of the **International Ladies Garment Workers Union** in San Antonio.

During the 1930s, Tenayuca served as the executive secretary of the **Workers Alliance of America**, a national communist organization. She helped organize several local chapters in San Antonio. Her high visibility in labor disputes made her an enemy of government officials and business owners.

Prior to one Communist party rally in San Antonio, local leaders instigated a riot in an effort to discredit Tenayuca. The U.S. House Un-American Activities Committee placed her on its blacklist for her Communist affiliations.

Tenayuca managed to persevere, and in the 1930s, she led the famous pecan shellers' strike. Texas was a leading producer of pecans, but many of the workers were Mexicans who received wages at barely subsistence levels, and they suffered in sweatshop-like conditions. When the United Cannery, Agricultural, Packing and Allied Workers of America replaced her as the leader of the strike because of her communist connections, she was "reinstated" as the honorary leader by the workers, due to her popularity.

In spite of her professed loyalty to her native state—Tenayuca described herself as "a Texan first and a Hispanic second"—she was a staunch advocate for the rights of Hispanic-Americans. She responded to U.S. immigration officials' unjust deportation of Mexican-American activists by staging protests and embarking on an aggressive letter-writing campaign. Her efforts helped bring more money to San Antonio from the federal New Deal program to create jobs for Spanish-speaking people.

During the pecan shellers' strike, Tenayuca met and fell in love with **Homer Brooks**, a fellow communist. They married and carried on their activism together. In 1939, they published an analysis of Mexican-American relations. Their study, "**The Mexican Question in the Southwest**," advocated for educational and cultural equality as the means to improve the plight of Mexicans in the region.

At the outset of World War II, Tenayuca left the Communist party in protest when the Soviet Union signed a nonaggression treaty with Adolf Hitler. She moved to San Francisco, where she earned her master's degree and became a school teacher. Eventually, Tenayuca returned to San Antonio, where she lived and worked for the remainder of her life.

Emma Tenayuca

During his lengthy career in politics, **Edward Roybal** was known to many as "the Dean of California's Latino Legislators" because of his pioneering efforts on behalf of Hispanics, first locally, and later on the national level.

Roybal was born in Albuquerque, New Mexico, the oldest of eight children of a hard-working railroad man. When Roybal was a boy, his mother gave him a necktie, which he wore wherever he went, because it symbolized what he wanted to become when he grew up—an educated professional.

Roybal graduated from high school during the Great Depression, and to help support his family, he went to work for the **Civilian Conservation Corps**, a federal government program designed to employ young men from 18 to 25. Later, he enrolled at the University of California at Los Angeles, where he earned his degree in business administration.

After serving in the U.S. Army during World War II, he returned to California and became the director of health education for the **Los Angeles County Tuberculosis and Health Association**.

In 1947, Roybal made an unsuccessful run for the L.A. City Council. In the aftermath of his defeat, he helped found the **Community Service Organization** (CSO). The group eventually became prominent in the Hispanic civil rights movement, and the training ground for such notable civil rights leaders as **César Chávez** (see no. 47) and **Dolores Huerta** (see no. 55).

In 1949, with the help of voter registration and get-out-the-vote drives organized by CSO, Roybal won a seat on the **L.A. City Council**, becoming the first Latino to hold that position in the 20th century. After four terms on the council, he won a seat in the **U.S. Congress** in 1962, becoming the first Hispanic Congressman from California since **Romualdo Pacheco** (see no. 14) in 1879.

While in Congress, Roybal authored the first bill to create and support bilingual programs in public schools. He also introduced legislation to provide bilingual proceedings in courts to help eliminate discrimination in the legal system. In 1976, he became one of the founding members of the **Congressional Hispanic Caucus**, which he later chaired. While the chair, he led the opposition to a bill that imposed sanctions on United States employers who hired illegal immigrants.

Roybal was also a strong advocate for legislation to aid the elderly, mentally disabled, and veterans. He sponsored and supported bills to eliminate age discrimination, create housing and community care facilities for seniors, provide mental health care programs, and create jobs for war veterans.

In 1992, Roybal retired from Congress, after serving for 30 years. His daughter, **Lucille Roybal-Allard** (see no. 70), won the election to replace him that same year.

Edward Roybal

Desi Arnaz is best known as the comic sidekick to his wife, **Lucille Ball,** in the tremendously popular television sitcom "I Love Lucy." He was also one of the greatest pioneers of Latin music in the United States. And perhaps more than any other Latin entertainer, he also helped shatter negative Hispanic stereotypes in the United States.

Arnaz was born in Santiago, Cuba. He and his mother came to the United States when he was only 16. After arriving in America, he joined the big band of the great **Xavier Cugat** (see no. 26), who was riding a wave of popularity for the Latin dance craze, the rumba. Arnaz played with Cugat's band briefly, then moved to Miami, Florida and started his own band.

Arnaz is largely credited with popularizing another Latin dance, the conga, which originated in Cuba. Although the dance was already known in America, he transformed it into a popular step that brought partygoers out of their seats.

In 1939, Arnaz was asked to act and sing in a Broadway musical, *Too Many Girls*. A year later, he starred in the film version, where he met a beautiful young actress, Lucille Ball. The two fell in love and married that same year.

After the 1940s, success for Arnaz came less from music than it did from film and television. He appeared in several movies, and in the 1950s, he and his wife became permanent fixtures in American culture with their hit television show, "I Love Lucy." The program was one of television's first sitcoms, and one of the most successful of all time; reruns are still being shown after more than 50 years.

Although audiences were drawn to the show for the hilarious antics of Lucille Ball, the show was also significant for the way it portrayed its Hispanic male character. Arnaz basically played himself—he was Ball's hus-

band, bandleader **Ricky Ricardo**. His character broke some previous stereotypes of Latin males in film and television. Ricardo was not a villain or a peasant. Instead, he was a likable and trustworthy middle-class husband and businessman—like many of the Anglo men who watched the show.

Desi Arnaz

The show was also significant because Arnaz and Ball produced it themselves. When the major studios were not interested in the concept, the couple formed their own company, **Desilu Productions**, to produce their show. The company eventually became a powerful financial force in Hollywood, producing numerous other television programs.

In 1960, Arnaz and Ball divorced. Arnaz sold his share of Desilu Productions to his ex-wife and slowly withdrew from show business. He made his last appearance in a movie, *The Escape Artist,* in 1982, four years before his death.

As a champion for the rights of undocumented Mexican workers in the United States, **Bert Corona** carried on his father's revolutionary passion in his own activism.

Corona's father had been a commandant in Pancho Villa's army during the Mexican Revolution at the turn of the 20th century. When Villa was defeated, Corona's parents moved to El Paso, where Corona was born. After his birth, his father returned to Mexico, and was killed there by Villa's enemies.

Bert Corona

After high school, Corona moved to Los Angeles to attend the University of Southern California. He worked there, too, and he became president of Local 26 of the **International Longshoreman and Warehouse Union**. The experience contributed to his views about Mexicans as an exploited class in the United States, views that guided him as an activist for the rest of his life.

Corona envisioned Mexican labor as a potentially powerful political force, and he believed that grass-roots organizing would achieve that end. Through his union involvement, he became active in the **Congress of Industrial Organizations** (CIO), and he became a leader in several groups that were allied with the CIO: the Congress of Spanish-Speaking Peoples, the Mexican-American Movement, and the Associacion Nacional Mexicano Americano, all three of which fought for the rights of Mexican-American workers.

Corona believed that undocumented Mexican workers were the most heavily exploited of all workers, and although labor unions were hostile to them, he championed their cause. He later formed the **Centro de Accion Social Autonomo** (CASA) to fight for the rights of immigrants.

Corona worked with **César Chávez** (see no. 46), fighting for the rights of farm-workers. They called for an end to the bracero program, which brought Mexican workers into the United States to work on farms, with harsh living conditions and extremely low wages. Corona also sought to organize the bracero workers, which later led to a rift with Chávez, when growers tried to use undocumented workers to undermine Chávez's fledgling United Farm Workers Union (UFW). Chávez and the UFW later adopted a policy of organizing all workers.

Later, Corona became involved in party politics. In 1959, he co-founded the **Mexican-American Political Association**. He was the California co-chair for the presidential campaigns of Lyndon Johnson (1964) and Robert Kennedy (1968), and he was involved in the founding of the **La Raza Unida Party** in 1970.

As perhaps his greatest legacy, Corona founded the **Hermandad Mexicana Nacional** (HMN) in 1951. The not-for-profit organization, which aids Latino immigrants in the United States, eventually grew to more than 30,000 member families. Corona served as National Director and Executive Director of the organization until his death.

José Yglesias, the "**Father of Cuban-American Literature**," was born in Ybor City, Florida to a Cuban mother and a Spanish father. He was raised by his mother from the age of two, after his father returned to his native town in Spain to recuperate from a debilitating illness, and died a few years later.

Due in part to the absence of his father, Yglesias was primarily self-educated. Ybor City (present-day Tampa) was home to a large community of laborers who worked as hand rollers in the local cigar factories. The workers formed a unique community with a proud sense of Hispanic literature, history, culture, and politics. Yglesias's youthful experiences in the community helped shape his identity, and served as the focal point of his writing as an adult.

After high school, Yglesias moved to New York City. He served in the U.S. Navy during World War II, then attended Black Mountain College in North Carolina, but he only stayed there for a year. In 1947, he moved back to New York, took a job with a pharmaceutical company, married, and started a family.

Yglesias possessed a passion for literature, and although he eventually became an executive of the company where he worked, he never gave up on his dream. In the 1950s, when he was in his 30s, and at an age when most men have become comfortable with their careers, he began to pursue his life's ambition.

Yglesias started out writing reviews and articles for various magazines. Then, in 1963, he published his first novel, *A Wake in Ybor City*, which would become a classic. This highly autobiographical novel introduced American readers to the peculiar world of the cigar workers. The book portrayed the tensions between Cuban and American cultures, as well as describing what made this community of workers unique. With the publication of this novel, Yglesias became the first Cuban-American creative writer to be published by a mainstream press. More importantly, the novel was a landmark work because it introduced the Cuban-American voice to American literature, thereby earning Yglesias the title of "Father of Cuban American Literature."

A Wake in Ybor City launched Yglesias's career as a writer. He soon became a full-time story contributor to popular magazines such as the *New Yorker* and the *Atlantic Monthly*. He also authored numerous nonfiction books about Spain and Cuba. Yglesias also wrote several more novels, most of which reflected on the difficult existence of Hispanics in the United States, and in particular, on life in his hometown's cigar worker community.

Cuban tobacco workers

José P. Martínez was an unlikely military hero. He was born in Taos, New Mexico, and as a young man during **World War II**, he was drafted into the army in Colorado, and was shipped to **Attu Island** in the Aleutian archipelago.

This chain of small islands off the coast of Alaska had become a key battleground between the United States and Japan. It was strategically located between the continents of North America and Asia, and the Japanese had seized three of the islands, which gave them a logistical advantage in their advance on the North American continent.

In 1943, the U.S. Army waged a protracted battle to eliminate the Japanese from the remote and snow-bound Attu Island. Repeatedly, the American forces failed to conquer a strategic pass where the Japanese had positioned themselves and were launching assaults. Martínez, only a private—the lowest rank a soldier can hold—took it upon himself to act.

Alone, he began to climb the steep, rocky hillside toward the enemy forces. From the top of the mountain, the Japanese fired down on him and the other Americans with machine guns, rifles, and mortars. Martínez advanced with only his Browning automatic rifle and a few hand grenades. Repeatedly, he stopped, turned around, and shouted at his fellow soldiers to advance with him. Some did; others did not have the courage.

Martínez reached the first line of Japanese defense and fought the enemy off with his rifle and grenades. He continued to advance up the steep, 150-foot mountainside, all the while under fire from Japanese troops positioned behind rocks and snow trenches to the side and in front of him. As he progressed, other American soldiers gained their courage and joined the charge. Along the way, Martínez destroyed several Japanese strongholds.

Finally, Martínez reached the top of the pass where the Japanese were entrenched. He ascended the ridge and encountered the last stronghold of the enemy. He fired on them, but he was overwhelmed by their firepower and was killed.

However, Martínez's efforts were not in vain. He had instigated an advance that eventually enabled the U.S. forces to recapture the pass and ultimately to expel the Japanese from the island. By driving them out of the Aleutian Islands, the United States was able to prevent the Japanese from making a land advance into the North American continent.

Martínez was recognized for his extreme bravery, leadership, and ultimate sacrifice. He was awarded a posthumous **Medal of Honor** by Congress for his "conspicuous gallantry and intrepidity above and beyond the call of duty." He was the first draftee in World War II to receive this distinguished honor.

Medal of Honor

Known to millions of television viewers as Mr. Roarke from the hit show "Fantasy Island," **Ricardo Montalbán** has had successful acting careers in the United States and Mexico. After experiencing the indignity of playing various ethnic roles, he has worked to improve the image of Latinos in American movies and television.

Montalbán was born in Mexico City, the youngest of four children. At the age of 17, he went to work in his father's dry goods store, but he had dreams of something bigger. He soon quit his job and moved to California, where his older brother lived.

In California, Montalbán enrolled in high school and signed up for drama classes, where he attracted the attention of film scouts looking for Latino types. The attention sparked his interest, and he decided to pursue an acting career.

Montalbán and his brother, who was an aspiring dancer, took a trip to New York City in 1940. Montalbán auditioned for several parts, and got his big break when he won a small role in the hit Broadway play, *Her Cardboard Lover*. Soon after, he returned to Mexico City to care for his ailing mother. There he capitalized on his American success to launch a film career.

Montalbán remained in Mexico throughout the years of World War II, making several successful movies. He then returned to the United States and signed a long-term contract with **Metro-Goldwyn-Mayer** studios (MGM). He stayed with MGM for nine years, mostly portraying the stereotypical role of suave Latin lovers.

All the while he was making films for MGM, Montalbán continued to perform on stage. He garnered national attention with his critically acclaimed roles in *Don Juan in Hell*, *The King and I*, and *Accent on Youth*. His

stage fame helped him land a job doing television commercials for Chrysler automakers.

Montalbán made a number of movies, some successful and some not, throughout the 1960s and '70s. In 1969, Montalbán and several others founded **Nosotros**, an organization dedicated to increasing opportunities for, and improving the image of, Latinos in the film profession. He was chosen the first president of the organization.

Then in 1978, he was chosen for the part of Mr. Roarke in the television show "Fantasy Island." The character served as the host of a fictitious island where guests traveled to live out their fantasies. It was a popular series and ran until 1985.

In 1979, Montalbán won an Emmy Award for his role as an Indian in the television miniseries "How the West Was Won." In 1988, he received the Golden Aztec Award from the **Mexican-American Opportunity Foundation** for his contributions to the cultural and social improvement of Mexican-Americans.

Ricardo Montalbán

Alicia Alonso
(1921–)

Alicia Alonso battled personal health problems and the political entanglements of the Cold War to become an internationally renowned ballet star.

Born Alicia Ernestina de la Caridad del Cobre Martínez in Havana, Cuba, she studied dance as a young girl, and made her first public appearance in *Sleeping Beauty* at the age of ten. In 1937, she moved to New York with her new husband, **Fernando Alonso**, where they both pursued professional dance careers. In 1939, she joined the **American Ballet Theater** and was given several solo parts, in acknowledgment of her talent.

Alonso's ascension to stardom was cut short in the late 1930s when she suffered detached retinas in both eyes. She underwent three operations and was confined to bed for a year. She recovered, and in 1943, danced *Giselle*, the role that would make her famous, at New York's **Metropolitan Opera House**. She performed that role for three years, and was promoted to principal dancer.

In 1948, Alonso returned to Cuba, where she and her husband founded their own ballet company. **The Ballet Alicia Alonso** provided a showcase for talent from throughout Latin America. In 1950, she also founded **Alicia Alonso Academy of Ballet**, to teach young dancers in Cuba. However, in 1956, a conflict with the government over the lack of funding prompted her to shut down the company and the school.

In 1957, Alonso demonstrated her international popularity when she became the first Western dancer to be invited to perform in the Soviet Union. The Cold War was at its peak, and few westerners traveled behind the Iron Curtain, let alone danced to adoring audiences there. Alonso performed for several months in Moscow, Leningrad, and other cities, and made an appearance on Soviet television.

After her trip, Alonso returned to the United States; in 1959, she returned to Cuba, after the communists rose to power. **Fidel Castro** gave her the financial support to reopen her academy and her company, which was renamed the **Ballet Nacional de Cuba**. Her efforts were successful, but the U.S. government banned her American performances because of her support for Castro's communist regime.

Eventually, the United States allowed Alonso to return, which she did in 1971. She made a number of performances, which won over audiences and critics, who were unaware that she had danced in a state of near blindness. Later, she had her vision restored again. In 1990, Alonso performed the pas de deux from *Swan Lake* with the American Ballet Theater, at the age of 69.

Alicia Alonso

Antonia Pantoja transformed an early childhood experience with labor struggles into a lifetime of service to poor and uneducated Puerto Ricans.

Born in Puerta de Tierra, San Juan, Pantoja lived in the barrio with her grandparents. Her grandfather was a cigar maker and a union organizer at the America Tobacco Company. His commitment to the fight for the workers' rights affected her, and she has spent her life dedicated to the cause of the empowerment of Puerto Ricans.

In the early 1940s, Pantoja graduated from the University of Puerto Rico and took a job as a teacher. The pay was low, and she decided to move to the U.S. mainland, where she settled in Brooklyn, New York. Since she could not find work as a teacher, she took a job in a lamp factory; soon, she was helping the workers—most of whom were also Puerto Rican—organize into a union.

In 1952, Pantoja earned her bachelor's degree in presocial work from Hunter College, and enrolled at Columbia University's School of Social Work, where in 1954 she earned her master's degree. At Columbia, she helped form a group that volunteered their time cleaning up Puerto Rican neighborhoods and assisting residents to register to vote.

In 1953, Pantoja and some of her student friends formed the **Puerto Rican Association for Community Affairs** (P.R.A.C.A.), which provided services and civic leadership training to the Puerto Rican community. In 1958, Pantoja and a group of beginning professionals organized the **Puerto Rican Forum, Inc.**, an agency designed to promote business and career development. The Forum, in turn, led to the creation of Pantoja's dream, the **Aspira Club of New York**. The club's purpose is to promote higher education for Puerto Ricans. Pantoja spent much of the 1960s working to expand Aspira into the schools of New York City and Puerto Rico.

In 1970, while completing work for her doctorate, Pantoja drafted a proposal for a university that would serve Puerto Ricans in the Unites States. In 1973, the proposal became reality, and Pantoja became the first chancellor of the **Universidad Boricua** in Washington, D.C.

Antonia Pantoja

During the mid-1970s, Pantoja relocated to San Diego, California where she took a job as associate professor at the Graduate School of Social Work, at California Sate University, San Diego.

During the 1980s, Pantoja returned to Puerto Rico and helped develop **Producir, Inc.** The company teaches self-sufficiency and community organization to help create jobs in the local economy.

Throughout her long career, Pantoja has been the recipient of many honors and awards, and in 1996, she became the first Puerto Rican woman to receive The Presidential Medal of Freedom, the nation's highest award for civilians.

43. Tito Puente
(1923–2000)

A multi-talented musician, as well as a prolific recording artist, **Tito Puente** was one of the most important figures in Latin music in the 20th century.

Puente was born Ernest Anthony Puente Jr. in New York City's Spanish Harlem. His parents had immigrated to the United States from Puerto Rico shortly before he was born.

As a boy, Puente dreamed of becoming a dancer, until he injured his ankle in a bicycle accident. His love for dance later influenced his style as a songwriter and a bandleader. As part of his musical education, Puente studied piano when he was young. Later, at the age of ten, he took up percussion.

Puente's talent as a drummer quickly blossomed. He was soon playing professionally at dances, and at the age of 15, he quit school

Tito Puente

and moved to Miami, Florida where he joined a band.

Puente served in the U.S. Navy during World War II. After the war ended, he took advantage of the American G.I. Bill, which provided college scholarships for war veterans. He used the money to attend the famous **Julliard School of Music** in New York City.

In 1948, Puente formed his own band, the **Piccadilly Boys**. They played regularly at the famous New York City venue, the **Palladium.** During this time, Puente and his band helped introduce the nation to a Cuban style of music known as the **mambo**, which is a fast, staccato, Afro-Cuban style of dance. During the 1930s, '40s, and '50s, this and other forms of Latin dance music, such as the rumba, cha-cha, conga, and merengue, enjoyed enormous popularity in the United States. Collectively, this type of music is often referred to as **salsa**, and Puente, along with **Xavier Cugat** (see no. 26), **Desi Arnaz** (see no. 36), and others, helped usher in the craze. In the 1950s, Puente was considered "**the King of Latin Music**" for his ability to appeal to Latin and Anglo audiences.

After the mambo craze, Puente turned his musical interest to jazz. In combining elements of Latin and jazz music, Puente helped pioneer yet another music craze, **Latin jazz**.

Puente was an innovative and entertaining bandleader. He introduced the timbal and the vibraphone to Afro-Cuban music. He played the piano, congas, bongos, and saxophone and would thrill audiences with his exciting solos. During his career, he recorded an unprecedented 100 albums, wrote more than 400 songs, and won four Grammy Awards.

Puente and his wife, Margie, had three children. He died in May 2000 at the age of 77, after undergoing heart surgery.

44. Celia Cruz
(1924–2003)

The so-called **Queen of Salsa** was born in Havana, Cuba. While she refused to divulge the exact year of her birth, it is believed to be 1924.

When she was a young girl, **Celia Cruz** sang lullabies to the smaller children in her house, and neighbors came to listen to her wonderful voice. Although her family wanted her to become a teacher, her signing talents were irrepressible, and she eventually convinced them to allow her to pursue a career in music. They consented, on one condition—that an older woman accompany her on all her performances.

In the 1940s, Cruz started singing professionally on Cuban radio programs. In 1947, she enrolled at **Havana's Conservatory of Music**, where she studied for three years. Then in 1950, she became the lead singer for the dance band **La Sonora Matancera**, which was the most popular dance band in Cuba. Shortly thereafter, she made her first recordings.

When Fidel Castro's Communists led a revolution that toppled the Cuban government in 1959, Cruz and the other members of La Sonora Matancera fled to the United States. The band continued to perform, but success was illusive. Latin sounds, such as the rumba and the conga, had been popularized years earlier in the United States by such great performers as **Xavier Cugat** (see no. 26) and **Tito Puente** (see no. 43). However, Cruz's

Celia Cruz

band could not break the grip of rock-'n'-roll, whose popularity eclipsed that of all other forms of music throughout the 1960s.

Cruz continued to perform, though, and by working with various African and Cuban rhythms, she helped popularize a new form of music known as salsa. Through her work, she helped the sounds of Latin music make a comeback in the United States.

In 1966, Cruz left La Sonora Matancera to join the orchestra of Tito Puente, with whom she continued to perform for many years. From there she embarked on a career as one of the world's greatest and most popular singers. Her career spanned more than five decades, during which she produced more than 70 albums, won numerous Grammy and other musical awards, and performed in electrifying concerts around the world. In addition to her powerful voice, she was also known for her gaudy costumes, musical improvisation, and boundless energy.

Some of Cruz's best-selling albums include "La Incomparable Celia" ("The Incomparable Celia") and "Feliz Encuentro" ("Happy Reunion"). In addition to her own fame, the popularity she created for salsa paved the way for numerous other performers, such as **Gloria Estefan** (see no. 95), to have successful careers in this unique musical form.

Romana Acosta Banuelos has lived the American Dream. She escaped poverty in an Arizona mining town, started two successful businesses, and served under President **Richard Nixon** as **Treasurer of the United States**.

Banuelos was born in Arizona, but her Mexican family returned to their native country when she was a girl. During the Depression, Arizona state officlas told Mexican families to return to Mexico because there were no jobs for them in the United States. The state offered to pay the expenses of families to travel to the Mexican border, and it promised they could return when the Depression ended.

Banuelos's family moved to Sonora, where she and her family worked on a ranch owned by relatives. They farmed crops that her father planted—wheat, corn, potatoes, and peanuts. In addition to farming, the young Banuelos

Romana Acosta Banuelos

helped her mother make empanadas, which they sold to local stores and bakeries.

Banuelos was a divorced mother of two sons by the time she was 19 years old. After her marriage ended, she returned to the United States with 36 cents in her purse. She took odd jobs, such as laundress and dishwasher, earning as little as $1 a day, and began to save her money.

In 1949, Banuelos pooled her $400 savings with some additional money from her aunt to open a tortilla factory in downtown Los Angeles. With their initial investment, they purchased a tortilla machine, a grinder, and a fan. They made $39 on the first day of business.

By the 1960s, **Ramona's Mexican Food Products** was a booming business, and it continued to grow. In 1979, the company—named after Ramona, an early California folk heroine—had 400 employees and distributed 22 different food products, with annual sales of more than $12 million. By 1990, it was the largest independent Mexican food processing plant in the state of California.

In 1965, Banuelos joined with several partners to found the **Pan-American National Bank** in East Los Angeles. It is the only bank in the United States owned and operated by Mexican-Americans. It was founded on the philosophy that if Mexican-Americans increase their financial base, they will also increase their political influence. What started as a small operation run from a trailer soon grew into a thriving business.

President Richard Nixon recognized Banuelos's accomplishments by appointing her U.S. treasurer in 1971. She was the highest-ranking Mexican-American in the Nixon administration, and the first Hispanic woman to hold such a high post. Banuelos resigned as treasurer in 1974 to spend more time with her business and her family.

Reies López Tijerina
(1926–)

In sharp contrast to other 1960s civil rights leaders who advocated nonviolent tactics, **Reies López Tijerina** employed confrontational and dangerous methods. His actions raised awareness of the long-neglected issue of **land grants** in the American Southwest.

Tijerina was born near Falls City, Texas. His parents worked as migrant farm- workers, and he attended numerous schools as they traveled throughout Texas. His mother gave him a religious upbringing and he enrolled in Bible school at the age of 18.

In the late 1950s, after spending several years as a traveling preacher, Tijerina developed a strong interest in the issue of land grants. Many Mexican-Americans had long argued that their claims to land in the Southwest under the previous Mexican, and before that Spanish, governments were denied and ignored when the land became part of the United States. Tijerina saw a connection between this injustice and the hardships facing Mexican-Americans.

In 1963, he founded the **Alianza Federal de Pueblos Libres** (Federal Alliance of Free Towns), whose mission was to seek redress for the usurpation of land. Within three years, the group had attracted more than 20,000 members. However, it failed to interest either the U.S. or Mexican governments in hearing its grievances; so, together with several hundred followers, Tijerina took action. He led an occupation of an area in New Mexico's **Kit Carson National Forest** and named it the **Republic of San Joaquin**. When police and forest rangers approached, Tijerina's group arrested them for trespassing.

This bold action resulted in federal charges being filed against Tijerina and others. It also opened a rift in the Hispanic civil rights movement. Some in the movement supported Tijerina's efforts; others strongly objected.

Reies López Tijerina

In 1967, several members of the Alliance were arrested, and Tijerina led an armed raid on the courthouse in New Mexico where they were being held. He and his forces freed their allies, but all of them were later captured by police and arrested.

In 1969, while he was free on bail, Tijerina attempted another takeover of the Kit Carson National Forest. He was arrested again and charged with pointing a gun at officers, who allegedly threatened his wife.

Tijerina was acquitted of the charges stemming from the raid that freed his fellow members, but he was convicted for the attempted forest takeover and served two years in prison. He was paroled in 1971, on the condition that he give up his position in the Alliance.

In 1976, after his parole ended, Tijerina resumed the presidency of the Alliance. He continued to advocate for the land rights issue well into the 1980s, but his following gradually disappeared. In the 1990s, he moved to Mexico.

César Chávez
(1927–1993)

Through his lifelong dedication to the cause of farmworkers, **César Chávez** became the most revered figure in the history of the Hispanic-American civil rights movement.

Chávez knew well the struggles of migrant farmworkers. One of five children, he was born on a farm owned by his parents in Yuma, Arizona. His parents were the children of Mexican immigrants. His family lost the farm when he was ten years old and moved to Oxnard, California, where they became migrant farmworkers.

In 1942, Chávez's father was injured in an accident and could no longer work, so Chávez left school and became a full-time farmworker. He had obtained only an eighth grade education after attending nearly 40 schools because of the family's migrant status.

César Chávez

During the 1950s, Chávez became involved in the **Community Service Organization**, an advocacy group for Mexicans and Mexican-Americans. He became general director, then resigned from the organization over its lack of interest in forming a farmworkers' union.

In 1962, Chávez took his lifetime savings of $1,200 and formed the **National Farm Workers Association**, in Delano, California. He spent the next several years canvassing the fields of California's Central Valley, encouraging farmworkers to join the union.

In 1965, Chávez's union joined another union in a strike against growers. The strike captured headlines, and **La Causa** (The Cause), had been born. Over the next 30 years, Chávez utilized the successful techniques of other labor unions, and the teachings of **Martin Luther King Jr**. and **Mahatma Gandhi**, to lead an impressive movement. He adhered to a firm belief in nonviolence, and through marches, rallies, and boycotts, he won the support of political leaders and the general public.

More importantly, numerous growers agreed to recognize the National Farm Workers Association as the representative of workers. The union became an affiliate of the AFL-CIO and, in 1972, became the **United Farm Workers**, or UFW. It became the largest union of agricultural workers in California, and at one point had more than 50,000 members.

Chávez believed the "truest act of courage...is to sacrifice ourselves in a totally nonviolent struggle for justice." He endured several fasts, one lasting 36 days, to call attention to La Causa. In 1975, California lawmakers created the **Agricultural Labor Relations Act**, which gave farmworkers the right to organize and negotiate for better wages and working conditions.

Chávez was an inspiration to millions, even those who never worked in the fields. When he died in 1993, more than 30,000 mourners marched through the streets of Delano, where his funeral was held. In 2000, California Governor Gray Davis signed a law designating March 31, Chávez's birthday, as a state holiday.

48. Lauro F. Cavazos
(1927–)

Born on a ranch, a sixth-generation Texan, **Lauro Fred Cavazos** rose from humble surroundings to become a prominent **scientist** and **educator**.

Cavazos was born on the King Ranch, where his father worked, but he aspired to be more than a ranch hand. He attended Texas Technological University, now Texas Tech, where he earned his B.A. and M.A. in zoology, in 1949 and 1952, respectively. In 1954, he earned his Ph.D. in physiology from Iowa State University.

After earning his doctorate, Cavazos taught anatomy at Texas Tech and later at the Medical College of Virginia and Tufts University in Massachusetts. He was appointed dean of the School of Medicine at Tufts.

Cavazos became an authority on anatomy, and authored numerous books and journal articles on the subject. He became involved in a number of organizations, including the American Association of Anatomists, the Endocrine Society and the Histochemical Society, the American Association for the Advancement of Science, the Pan American Association of Anatomy, and the World Health Organization. He has also served as editor of a number of medical journals.

Cavazos became committed to education, and in particular to the cause of educating Hispanic students. His concern was that Hispanics have traditionally suffered disproportionately high dropout rates, based on their overall student numbers in American schools.

In 1980, Cavazos returned to his alma mater, Texas Tech, as the president of the university and its Health Sciences Center. He was the first Hispanic, and the first graduate of Texas Tech, to hold these titles.

In 1988, President **Ronald Reagan** made Cavazos the first Hispanic-American to serve in a presidential cabinet by appointing him **Secretary of the Department of Education**.

While serving in this post, Cavazos continued to emphasize the importance of educating Hispanics and other minorities. Through his leadership, the **President's Council on Educational Excellence for Hispanic-Americans** was formed to create scholarships for Latino youths.

President Reagan chose Cavazos because of his credentials and his strong dedication, although the two men belonged to different parties—Reagan was a Republican and Cavazos a Democrat. It is rare for a president to select people who belong to the opposing party for his cabinet. However, Cavazos performed so well in his post that Reagan's Republican successor, **George Bush**, reappointed him.

Lauro Cavazos

In 1990, Cavazos resigned from the Department of Education and returned to teaching. He continued to serve as an adjunct professor at Tufts School of Medicine, and he worked as an educational and business consultant. In 1993, Cavazos joined the Board of Directors of Luby's Cafeteria, Inc., a Texas franchise; he retired from the board in 1999.

Called by many the "The First Lady of the Hispanic Theater," **Carmen Margarita Zapata** was born in New York City to a Mexican father and an Argentine mother. Growing up in the barrio of Spanish Harlem, she struggled early in school, as the family spoke only Spanish at home. As a girl, she took an interest in the arts, studying violin, singing in the school choir, and performing in school plays.

Carmen Zapata

In 1946, Zapata made her debut in the chorus of the hit Broadway musical, *Oklahoma*. She eventually earned a lead role in the production, and played principal roles in several other hit Broadway shows, such as *Bells Are Ringing* and *Guys and Dolls*. She continued to appear in musicals for another 20 years. At the same time, she also performed as Marge Cameron, a musical comedy act she created for appearances in nightclubs.

In 1967, Zapata decided to move to California. She obtained several roles in films, although they were mostly for stereotyped, negative Latina characters, such as prostitutes or maids. The offensive roles inspired her to act for change. She played a role in forming the initial minority committee of the Screen Actors Guild, and she helped **Ricardo Montalbán** (see no. 40) form the Hispanic actors organization, **Nosotros**.

Zapata eventually found success in television acting. Over the course of her career, she has made more than 300 television appearances, and has received three Emmy nominations. One of her most memorable roles, and the one of which she is most proud, was the character of Doña Luz, which she performed for nine years on the Public Broadcasting System's bilingual children's program, "Villa Alegre."

After she was asked to perform the lead role in the Spanish-language play *Cada quien su vida* (*To Each His Own*), Zapata discovered the beauty of performing works in the native language of her ancestors. She then became actively involved in efforts to introduce English-speaking audiences to Hispanic literature and theater. In 1973, she co-founded the **Bilingual Foundation of the Arts** (BFA) in Los Angeles, to provide the general public with the opportunity to experience Latino culture and theater. The BFA also designed **Teen Theater Project**, a theater education program for at-risk students. In the 1980s, Zapata was appointed by the estate of the great Spanish poet Federico García Lorca to translate his trilogy, *Blood Wedding, Yerma,* and *The House of Bernarda Alba*.

Zapata has received numerous awards and honors for her activism, and in 1990, she was given El Lazo de Dama de la Orden de Merito Civil (the Civil Order of Merit) by Juan Carlos I, King of Spain.

50. Reubén Salazar
(1928–1970)

A martyr for the Mexican-American civil rights movement, **Reubén Salazar** was one of the most prominent Hispanic journalists in the United States at the time of his tragic death.

Salazar was born in the Mexican city of Ciudad Juárez. Shortly after his birth, his family moved across the border to El Paso, Texas, where his father worked as a watch repairman. The young man went to high school there, then enlisted in the army. During that time, he also became an American citizen.

After the armed services, Salazar enrolled in the University of Texas at El Paso, where he earned his B.A. in 1954. At the university, he developed an interest in journalism, and he took a job as a reporter with the *Herald-Post* newspaper. He quickly demonstrated his skill as a journalist when he posed as a vagrant and was arrested. He wrote an exposé about his experience, which described the cruel conditions of El Paso prisons.

Salazar moved to California in the late 1950s. He worked for several newspapers, and in 1959, he took a job with the *Los Angeles Times*. At the Times, he achieved notoriety for his coverage of issues that were important to the Hispanic community. He also spent a year as a war correspondent in Vietnam, and for three years, he worked in the paper's Mexico City bureau, where he became the bureau chief.

Salazar returned to Los Angeles in 1968 and began writing a weekly column about Chicano affairs. The assignment began just as the Chicano movement was becoming an important and powerful force in the national civil rights effort. He also took a job as the news director for a Spanish-language television station, KMEX. For his reporting in print and on television, Salazar became a polarizing figure in the controversy surrounding discrimination of Hispanics. In particular, he was a fierce critic of the Los Angeles Police Department for its treatment of Mexican-Americans.

In August 1970, Salazar covered a protest in Los Angeles over the disproportionate number of Mexican-Americans who were fighting and dying in the Vietnam War. The event began peacefully, but according to some reports, police first incited the crowd, and then began to enforce strict crowd control. An officer fired a tear gas gun into a bar where Salazar was having a beer. The canister hit Salazar in the head and killed him. No officers were charged with his death, but many of Salazar's supporters felt it was not an accident. Salazar became a symbol for the injustices and abuses that Mexican-Americans had experienced at the hands of authorities.

Reubén Salazar

51. Richard "Pancho" Gonzales
(1928–1995)

Richard "Pancho" Gonzales broke down color and class barriers while becoming a dominant and exciting tennis player who drew unprecedented crowds to his sport.

Gonzales was born in South Central Los Angeles to poor working class parents who had emigrated from Mexico. When he was 12, his mother gave him a second-hand tennis racquet. He began hanging around the nearby public courts, watching the other players, observing their technique, and practicing late into the evening.

At the age of 14, with only two years of experience, the self-taught Gonzales earned the number one ranking in southern California for his age. Soon after, the Southern California Tennis Association (SCTA) suspended him for poor attendance at school.

Gonzales quit tennis and drifted into a life of delinquency. At 17, after a year in a juvenile hall, he joined the navy. The structured discipline of the armed forces did not suit his independent nature, though, and he was back home in a year.

In 1947, after a three-year layoff, and with only a few months of preparation, Gonzales reached the finals of the Southern California Tennis Championship, where he lost to Jack Kramer, the number one player in the nation.

Gonzales's impressive performance earned him a spot on the eastern amateur circuit. He performed remarkably well there and returned to California as the 17th-ranked player in the country. Again organized tennis suspended him, this time for a violation of an obscure rule.

Many Gonzales supporters believed that the all-white tennis establishment was determined to keep a young man of Mexican ancestry from breaking into the sport. Gonzales, however, remained undaunted. He improved his national ranking to eighth and won the National Clay Court Championship and the U.S. Lawn Tennis Championship. In 1948 and 1949, he won the U.S. National Championship, today known as the **U.S. Open.** Later in 1949, he turned professional.

Gonzales soon became the best player on the professional tour, and arguably the best player in the world. He remained dominant throughout the 1950s, winning the U.S. professional championship seven years in a row, from 1953 to 1959.

Gonzales drew immense crowds throughout his career. They came to see his graceful style of play and brilliant shot making, as well as his fiery temperament. His outsider status also attracted new fans to the staid, tradition-bound sport. His dominance and fan appeal helped propel tennis to a new level of popularity.

In 1968, Gonzales was inducted into the **International Tennis Hall of Fame**. The next year, as a 41-year-old grandfather, he won a first-round match at Wimbledon, at the time, the longest match in the tournament's history. He continued to play into the early 1970s, stretching his career over four decades.

Richard "Pancho" Gonzales

Boxer, businessman, poet, and civil rights organizer, **Rodolfo "Corky" Gonzales** became one of the most important leaders of the Chicano movement during the 1960s.

Born in Denver, Colorado, Gonzales was three years old when his mother died. He attended several schools as a boy, while his father migrated throughout the state taking work in coal mines and in the fields.

As a teenager, Gonzales became a skilled boxer. He won the national and international **Golden Gloves** championships and turned professional after high school. He had a winning career that lasted more than eight years.

After boxing, Gonzales became a businessman. He ran a tavern in Denver, then a bail bond business, and later, an automobile insurance agency. During this time, he also got involved in politics and social service. He became a leader in the Democratic party and was considered a possible candidate for state or federal office, until 1966. That year he terminated all of his political involvement after a local newspaper accused him of discrimination in administering Denver's War on Poverty program.

Gonzales then became active in **La Raza**, the movement to win equality for Mexican-Americans in the United States. He formed an organization, **La Cruzada Para La Justicia** (the Crusade for Justice), whose objective was to secure civil rights and economic and political equality for Chicanos.

In 1967, Gonzales displayed his literary talents when he published *I Am Joaquín*, an epic poem that appeared in book form. It recalls the life of the slain Gold Rush era bandit and folk hero, **Joaquín Murieta** (see no. 15), as a metaphor for the plight of Mexican-Americans in the United States. It was arguably Gonzales's most important contribution to the cause, as it became an emblem for the movement.

Throughout the late 1960s, Gonzales was one of the national leaders of la raza. In 1968, he joined **Reies López Tijerina** (see no. 46) as one of the Hispanic leaders of the **Poor Peoples' March** to Washington, D.C. Gonzales also espoused many of the same views as Tijerina regarding self-determination and the need for a national homeland for people of Mexican descent in the Southwestern United States.

Rodolfo "Corky" Gonzales

In 1970, Gonzales formed the **Colorado La Raza Unida Party** (LRUP) and became its first state chairman. In 1972, he lost a power struggle with the chairman of the Texas LRUP, **José Angel Gutiérrez** (see no. 75), to become the first national chairman of the party.

Slowly, Gonzales retreated from the national spotlight as a civil rights leader. During the 1980s, he returned to boxing, as a promoter and trainer, although he continued to run the Crusade for Justice and speak out on civil rights issues.

Jaime Escalante

Born in La Paz, Bolivia, **Jaime Escalante** immigrated to the United States in the 1960s, seeking greater stability. What he found were new challenges and unexpected national fame.

Escalante was a successful teacher in his native country. He graduated from San Andrés University in La Paz, then taught math and science at high schools and the **Colegio Militar**, the national military academy.

When he came to the United States, Escalante's Bolivian credentials were not accepted, and he was forced to work at odd jobs, such as busboy, cook, and electrical technician, to earn a living. At the same time, he attended classes at Pasadena City College and later at California State University, Los Angeles, where he earned his bachelor's degree in mathematics in 1974. With his degree in hand, he was qualified to teach again.

Escalante deliberately sought the challenge of teaching kids in a rough Hispanic neighborhood, at **Garfield High School** in East Los Angeles. Little was expected of these students, by themselves or by others,

because of the difficult circumstances in which they lived.

Escalante employed tough street talk and an uncompromising, confrontational style that challenged the students to demand more of themselves. He appealed to their sense of pride in and curiosity about their culture by teaching them the mathematical brilliance of the ancient Mayan calendar system. He succeeded in getting them to pass their basic math courses and defied prevailing wisdom by introducing a calculus course. Most school officials believed calculus was too difficult for these students.

In 1982, Escalante proved his critics wrong again by having his students take the advanced placement (AP) calculus test, a rigorous exam, that can earn college credit for high school students. In a testament to his tremendous teaching ability, all of Escalante's students passed the test.

Some of his colleagues asserted that either a mistake had been made or the students had cheated. Escalante had his students take a new test. They performed even better the second time and silenced the disbelievers.

Escalante's accomplishments caught the attention of newspapers, magazines, and television. After reading a story about him in the *Los Angeles Times*, in 1988, Cuban-born director **Ramón Menéndez** made a popular film about Escalante called *Stand and Deliver*.

The movie made Escalante a national celebrity and a hero in the teaching community. He was featured on the PBS television program "**Futures**" and began working as an education consultant. He has received numerous honors. His students continued to excel, and many of them have received academic scholarships from colleges and universities. In 1991, Escalante moved to Sacramento, California, where he became a teacher at Hiram Johnson High School.

After emigrating from Cuba at the age of 15, **María Irene Fornés** became a successful playwright in the United States. She has produced plays on a variety of themes in English and Spanish. Her unusual characters and unconventional techniques make her one of the most innovative and creative playwrights in contemporary drama.

Born in Havana, Fornés came to the United States with her family after her father died. He had been an intellectual and a rebel, whose nonconformist ideas had a profound impact on her. She did not speak English when she came to America, and she got her first job working in a ribbon factory. Fornés eventually learned English and worked as a translator. Later, she got a job as a doll maker, and at the same time took up painting. In 1951, she became a naturalized citizen, and she spent the rest of the decade pursuing a career as a painter.

Fornés never achieved the fame she sought as a painter, but in 1960, she discovered a new passion that would prove to be her calling in life. She was assisting her roommate, an aspiring writer struggling with writer's block, when she discovered that she too had a strong interest in writing. The roommate, **Susan Sontag**, went on to become a famous philosopher and critic, and Fornés took up playwriting.

Fornés published her first play, *La Viuda* (*The Widow*) in 1961. She followed that the next year with her first produced play, *There! You Died*, which launched her into a prolific career. Over the course of her multi-decade career, Fornés has written and produced dozens of plays, which have won her numerous awards. She counts among her honors six **Obie Awards**, given for the year's best Off-Broadway shows. Her plays are renowned for their striking characters and creative forms.

She has been referred to as the "**Picasso of theater**" for her innovative and imaginative style. Two of her most popular plays are *Dr. Kheal* and *Fefu and Her Friends*.

Many of Fornés's plays reflect her Cuban origins. Several of them were written in Spanish and were produced by **International Arts Relations** (INTAR), the native Spanish theater of New York. *Lovers and Keepers* is a musical, produced in 1986, featuring music by among others, the famous Latin-jazz musician **Tito Puente** (see no. 43).

María Irene Fornés

In 1972, Fornés co-founded the **New York Theatre Strategy**, which for nearly a decade helped writers produce their plays. Fornés has been a dedicated teacher and helped numerous playwrights get their careers started.

Dolores Huerta
(1930–)

When **Dolores Huerta** was little, her grandfather gave her the nickname "seven tongues" because she was a talkative girl. It was sign of what she was to become.

Huerta was born Dolores Fernández in the small mining town of Dawson, New Mexico. Her father was a coal miner who later became involved in the labor movement and eventually entered politics as a state legislator.

Huerta's parents divorced when she was young, and she moved with her mother to Stockton, California. Her mother opened a restaurant and hotel, which also served as an impromptu emergency shelter whenever a farmworker suffered an injury on the job. It was here that Huerta first witnessed braceros (migrant farmworkers), who were treated "like dogs, almost like slaves," she said.

After attending college, Huerta became a teacher. Seeing the farmworkers' children come to class, in her words, "barefoot, so hungry, so poor," she decided she could do more to help her students as an activist who organized their parents.

In the early 1960s, Huerta became involved in the **Community Service Organization**, which advocated for the rights of Mexicans and Mexican- Americans. There she met **César Chávez** (see no. 47), who shared her concern about the plight of farmworkers. Eventually, they both left the CSO and

began to recruit farmworkers to form their own union.

It was not an easy task. Many of the braceros feared upsetting the powerful growers who employed them. However, Huerta and Chavez eventually succeeded in forming an effective union—later known as the **United Farm Workers** (UFW)—that fought for better wages and working conditions for its members. It won the support of college students, politicians, activists, and the public.

During her early years in the labor movement, Huerta met her second husband, Ventura Huerta, who was also an activist. The marriage did not last, partly as a result of her devotion to her work. Although she has admitted to placing her labor activities above concerns for her family, Huerta married twice, and managed to raise a total of 11 children.

In 1988, during a peaceful demonstration in San Francisco, Huerta suffered broken ribs and a ruptured spleen when police officers swung their batons at protesters. The incident made headlines and caused the San Francisco police to change their crowd control policies. Huerta recovered from her injuries and returned to work for the UFW.

Huerta continued to work for the UFW as its treasurer as she entered her seventies. Her concerns remained women's issues, in particular equal wages, improved education, day care, and health services.

Dolores Huerta

56. Marisol
(1930–)

Born in France to wealthy Venezuelan parents, **Marisol Escobar** became a nationally recognized painter and sculptor in the United States. She infused Latin American and native American elements into the **pop art movement** of the 1950s and '60s, using as her artistic name, Marisol.

In 1941, Marisol's mother died and her father moved the family to Los Angeles. As a teenager there, she took an interest in art. She was extremely gifted and moved back to Paris at the age of 19 to study at the prestigious Académie des Beaux Arts.

In the 1950s, after graduating from the Académie, Marisol relocated to New York City. She continued her art studies at the Art Students' League and at the New School for Social Research. She immersed herself in the New York art scene, which at the time was preoccupied with the impressionistic style of painting. She studied impressionistic painting and became friends with other artists, some of whom, like **Robert Rauschenberg** and **Jasper Johns**, later became her contemporaries in a new movement that came to be known as pop art.

Marisol quickly lost interest in impressionism and shifted her attention to the themes of Latin American and pre-Columbian **folk art**. She quit painting and took up sculpting, without any formal training, and began to incorporate elements of her heritage into her work.

Marisol soon distinguished herself as an innovative sculptor who used a variety of mediums, including carved wood, molded terra cotta, and welded metal. True to the pop art movement, of which she became one of the most well-known practitioners, her sculptures featured common, everyday materials, including used and recycled items, which she incorporated with an imaginative flair.

Marisol also became known for her eccentric behavior. She produced a number of self-por-

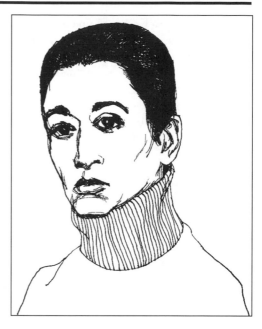

Marisol

traits and casts of her own body parts. Her reclusive lifestyle contributed to the reputation.

Marisol's success has spanned several decades. In 1967, the *London Telegraph Sunday Magazine* commissioned her to produce satiric sculptures of the British prime minister and the royal family. Later, she produced similar representations of U.S. President Lyndon Johnson, French President Charles de Gaulle, and Spain's Generalissimo Francisco Franco.

In the 1970s, Marisol produced one of her most famous works, relief sculptures of some of Leonardo da Vinci's paintings. Her impression of *The Last Supper* was praised by the critics. Marisol's works have appeared in, and been purchased for the permanent collections of, some of the most respected museums in the world. In 1991, she was honored by a display of her sculptures in the **National Portrait Gallery** in Washington, D.C.

Renowned prima ballerina **Lupe Serrano** had the advantage of growing up in a musical family. Her father was a Spanish-born musician from Argentina who met her mother while he was on tour in Mexico City. Serrano was born and raised in Santiago, Chile, where her father had conducted an orchestra and decided to settle.

When she was 13, Serrano's family moved to Mexico City, where her parents enrolled her in formal ballet training classes. She had been gifted with talent and a natural love for dance since she was a little girl, and her parents wanted to take advantage of the cultural opportunities the city had to offer. At the age of 14, she debuted in a Mexico City ballet company's production of *Les Sylphides*.

Serrano was so committed to dance that she finished high school early and began touring immediately, skipping college altogether. At the age of 18, she went on a tour of Central America and Colombia with the great Cuban ballerina **Alicia Alonso** (see no. 41). Upon her return, Serrano joined the government-sponsored Ballet Folklorika of Mexico but remained there only briefly. At the age of 20, she moved to New York City to advance her career.

Serrano quickly earned a position with the **Ballet Russe de Monte Carlo**, where she had her first solo performances. The company folded, and she returned to Mexico City to star in a television program about the arts.

In 1953, Serrano returned to New York to join the prestigious **American Ballet Theatre** (ABT) as a principal dancer. She performed with ABT for almost 20 years, in more than 50 different roles, including classics such as *Swan Lake* and *Giselle*. She traveled the world and won over sophisticated audiences in Europe and in the Soviet Union.

In 1957, Serrano married ABT conductor **Kenneth Schermerhorn**. They would have two daughters. Serrano continued to dance with the ABT after her children were born and when the family moved from New York to New Jersey to Milwaukee, as her husband took jobs with orchestras and symphonies in those cities.

When they moved to Milwaukee, Serrano began teaching at the University of Milwaukee and the Conservatory of Milwaukee. It was the beginning of her second profession. She retired from dancing in 1970, at the age of 40.

Serrano's marriage ended in divorce, but she remained in the United States to continue her teaching career. She has taught at the National Academy of Arts in Illinois and the Pennsylvania Ballet School in Philadelphia. In 1988, she was appointed artistic associate of the Washington, D.C. Ballet.

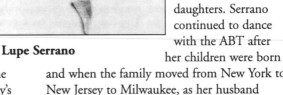

Lupe Serrano

58. Roberto C. Goizueta
(1931–1997)

The driving force behind the success of the **Coca-Cola Company** in the latter part of the 20th century, **Roberto C. Goizueta** became one of the most successful men in corporate America. His life story is a realization of the American Dream.

Goizueta was born and raised in Havana, Cuba. He came to the United States and attended Yale University in New Haven, Connecticut, where he earned his B.S. in chemical engineering in 1953. After college, he returned to Havana, where he took a position as a quality control chemist in the technical department of Compañia Embotelladora Coca-Cola, S.A., a wholly owned subsidiary of the Coca-Cola Company.

In the Cuban Communist revolution of 1959, Fidel Castro's forces took over the Havana Coca-Cola plant where Goizueta worked, forcing him to flee the country with his wife and children. Goizueta remained with Coca-Cola, and in 1964, he was assigned to the corporate offices in Atlanta, Georgia. The following year, he was named assistant to the vice president for research and development. Two years later, he was promoted to vice president of engineering. By 1981, he had climbed the ranks to become the company's CEO and chairman of the board.

Over the next 16 years, Goizueta presided over a number of the company's bold moves. In 1985, the company launched New Coke, which was a commercial failure, but Goizueta turned it into a positive when he relaunched Coca-Cola Classic just a few months later. In 1989, after the fall of the Berlin Wall, Coca-Cola expanded into Eastern European markets. The company made a deal with China in 1993. In that same year, the popular "Always Coca-Cola" ads were unveiled.

During Goizueta's tenure, the Coca-Cola Company's stock market value rose by 3,500 percent to $150 billion, and sales climbed to

$19 billion. Coca-Cola became the preeminent soft drink manufacturer in the world, with control of nearly half the world market.

In 1991, Goizueta was criticized for receiving an $86 million compensation package, but he defended his salary at the company's annual stockholders' meeting by pointing to the tremendous growth and profit he had brought to the company. None of the shareholders at the meeting could argue with him.

Goizueta helped bring the Olympic Games to Atlanta in 1996, and he was actively involved in community service. He served as a trustee of the Robert W. Woodruff Arts Center of Emory University and a board member of the Atlanta Symphony Orchestra. He was also a board member of the Boys Club of America and a founding director of the Points of Light Initiative Foundation.

Goizueta died in 1997 of lung cancer.

Roberto Goizueta (right) with Don Keough

Rita Moreno rose from poverty in Puerto Rico to build a highly successful career in show business. She has persistently fought against derogatory stereotypes of Latino women, and has won all four of the entertainment industry's most prestigious honors.

Born Rosa Dolores Alverio, in the small town of Humacao, Moreno came to New York with her divorced mother at the age of five. At 13, she left school to become an actress. Initially, she provided Spanish voiceovers for American movies. Then in 1950, after her first film appearance, Moreno signed a contract with Metro-Goldwyn-Mayer (MGM). The contract didn't last long, but her career was launched; over the next several decades, she would be featured in dozens of movies

Rita Moreno

Unfortunately, many of Moreno's roles were for stereotypical ethnic characters, including Arabs and American Indians, as well as Latinas. Her dark-skinned beauty, combined with some high profile romances,

only added to her reputation and image as a hot-blooded Latina.

Moreno's challenges affected her personally. She spent several months in psychotherapy trying to resolve issues about her ethnic identity, and in 1960, she attempted suicide by swallowing a bottle of sleeping pills. Fortunately, she recovered, and went on to star in the role that made her famous and changed her career.

In 1961, Moreno won an **Academy Award** for best supporting actress for her portrayal of Anita in the movie version of the hit Broadway play, *West Side Story*. The classic film depicted the lives of rival youth gangs—Puerto Rican immigrants and native Anglos—living in New York City. It won a total of ten Academy Awards.

From then on, Moreno's career improved dramatically. While she continued to star in movies, she also worked in the theater, and then moved on to television, as well. In 1975, she accepted a starring role in the Broadway hit play, *The Ritz*. In that production, she portrayed Googie Gomez, a spoof of the stereotypical Latina, the kind of character that she had long resisted. Audiences loved the satire, and she received a **Tony Award** for best featured actress.

A few years earlier, Moreno had won a **Grammy Award** for her vocal performance on the soundtrack for the children's television show, "The Electric Company." In the late 1970s, she also won two **Emmy Awards**, one for her appearance on "The Muppet Show" and another for her lead role in an episode of "The Rockford Files."

In 1965, Moreno married Dr. Leonard Gordon, a New York City cardiologist who eventually became her manager and partner. As she turned seventy, she continued to perform in plays around the country, often with her daughter, Fernanda.

Oscar de la Renta
(1932–)

It was a twist of fate that prompted **Oscar de la Renta** to detour from his intended career as a painter into the world of fashion design.

De la Renta was born in Santo Domingo, Dominican Republic. He began his art studies at the University of Santo Domingo and completed them at the Academia de San Fernando in Madrid, Spain.

De la Renta had dreamed of becoming an abstract painter, but while in Madrid, he took an interest in clothing design. He showed some of his design sketches to the wife of an American diplomat. She was so impressed that she asked him to design a dress for her daughter's society debut. When a photograph of the debutante wearing the dress appeared on the cover of *Life* magazine, de la Renta's career was launched.

De la Renta went to work for the Spanish designer **Balenciaga**. In 1961, de la Renta moved to Paris to become an assistant to **Antonio del Castillo** at the Lanvin-Castillo fashion house.

In 1963, de la Renta moved to the United States; eight years later, he became a U.S. citizen. After working for American designers, such as **Elizabeth Arden** and **Jane Derby**, in the early 1960s, de la Renta started his own company in 1965.

In 1967, de la Renta married his first wife, Françoise de Langlade, the former Editor-in-Chief of *Vogue* magazine's French edition. Over the next 15 years, de la Renta's clientele expanded greatly and his business thrived. De Langlade died in 1983, and in 1989, de la Renta married his second wife, Annette Reed.

De la Renta eventually became one of the most celebrated designers of elegant evening wear, including high fashion and ready-to-wear clothing, as well as perfumes and jewelry. A stylized designer, he has incorporated Hispanic elements into his clothing. De la

Renta attributes this to the legacy of his first mentor, Balenciaga, who he says created "the most beautiful folkloric clothes ever made."

De la Renta has used his financial success to help some of society's less fortunate, especially those in his native country. He co-founded **La Casa del Niño**, near his home in the Dominican Republic. It serves as an orphanage to 22 children, as well as a school and recreation center for 350 other children whose mothers work.

In the early 1990s, the renowned Paris fashion house **Balmain** invited de la Renta to become its chief designer. It was the first time an American designer had occupied such a prestigious position in the French fashion industry. De la Renta's first Balmain collection was unveiled in 1993 to high praise.

Oscar de la Renta

Born the youngest son in a large family in Carolina, Puerto Rico, **Roberto Clemente** rose to become one of the greatest baseball players of all time.

Clemente did not begin to play baseball until he reached high school. However, he caught on quickly, and in 1954, at the age of 19, he signed a contract with the **Brooklyn Dodgers** that included a $10,000 bonus.

Roberto Clemente

At the time, baseball's rules required that any player who received such a bonus must play in the major leagues or become eligible to be drafted by another team at the end of the year. The Dodgers could have kept Clemente had they placed him on their roster, but they sent him instead to their Montreal farm team. The Dodgers hoped that no other team would discover Clemente there, but he was difficult to hide. A scout for the **Pittsburgh Pirates** noticed his talent, and the team signed him at the end of the season. To the chagrin of Dodgers fans, Clemente played for the Pirates for his entire career.

Clemente played well in his first few seasons, but in the 1960s, he became a full-blown star. Pitchers feared his ability to hit pitches thrown even outside the strike zone. An outstanding right fielder, he was capable of throwing runners out at home plate from 420 feet away.

Clemente amassed a lifetime batting average of .317, in a career that spanned 18 seasons. He won the National League batting title four times, and in 1966, he was the League's Most Valuable Player. He was also selected to the NL All-Star team 12 times. In 1971, he gave an unforgettable performance in the World Series. Hitting a remarkable .414, and making a number of spectacular defensive plays, he led the underdog Pirates to the world championship. In the final game of the 1972 season, Clemente joined an elite group of players by getting his **3,000th career hit**.

Clemente was very conscious of his Latino heritage, and was deeply concerned about the plight of the poor in Latin America. He donated his earnings from product endorsements to charitable causes in Spanish-speaking countries, and he dreamed of opening a baseball clinic for the poor in Puerto Rico.

Clemente was tragically killed in a plane crash on New Year's Eve 1972. He was traveling on a cargo plane delivering relief supplies to Nicaraguan earthquake victims. Shortly after his death, Clemente was inducted into the **Baseball Hall of Fame** in a special election that waived the usual requirement of a five-year waiting period. In the 1970s, his dream was realized with the construction of the Roberto Clemente Sports City Complex in San Juan, Puerto Rico.

62. Nicholasa Mohr
(1935–)

Born Nicholasa Rivera-Golpe, **Nicholasa Mohr** was raised in New York City, along with her three brothers, by their Puerto Rican immigrant parents. When she was eight years old, Mohr's father died; her mother died when she was in high school.

As a young girl, Mohr developed an interest in drawing and painting, which provided her with an escape from the bigotry and discrimination she encountered in school. An excellent student, after graduating high school she attended the Art Students League in New York. Then she moved to Mexico City and attended the Taller de Gráfica Popular, where she studied the works of the great Mexican artists, such as **Diego Rivera**, **Frida Kahlo**, and **José Clemente Orozco**.

Mohr was inspired by the manner in which the paintings of these artists reflected their cultural identities. She then returned to New York and enrolled at the New School for Social Research, where she met her future husband, Irwin Mohr, who was a Ph.D. student in psychology. In 1959, she enrolled at the Brooklyn Museum Art School and the Pratt Center for Contemporary Printmaking.

By the late 1960s, Nicholasa Mohr had become a recognized painter in the art circles of New York. Then in the early 1970s, she developed an interest in writing. In 1973, Mohr published her first book, *Nilda*, a fictional, third-person account of her early years growing up in Spanish Harlem. The book received several awards for **juvenile fiction**, and it earned her numerous distinctions. It made her the first woman to write in English about the struggles of Puerto Ricans in New York, and it made her the first United States

Nicholasa Mohr

Hispanic woman in modern times to be published by a major commercial publisher.

Mohr followed up her first book with *El Bronx Remembered* in 1975 and *In Nueva York* in 1977, two more commercial and critical successes. She continued to publish throughout the 1970s, '80s, and '90s. In 1995, she published *Song of the Coquí and Other Tales of Puerto Rico*, a collection of folk stories for children. Her string of popular books has made her the most widely published Hispanic female in the United States.

All of Mohr's books reflect on the lives of Puerto Ricans in the barrios of New York City. In addition to writing, she has drawn the covers and illustrations for many of her books. She is a university professor, and she has worked as a television writer and producer. Her books often appear on the classroom reading lists for young adults.

63. Martha P. Cotera
(1938–)

As an activist, historian, and educator, **Martha Cotera** has spent her adult life empowering Hispanic men and women in Texas and raising the awareness of Hispanic issues in the general community.

Cotera was born in Nuevo Casa Grande, in the Mexican state of Chihuahua. Her family immigrated to El Paso, Texas in 1946. She went to school there and earned her bachelor's degree in English from the University of Texas at El Paso. Later, she earned her master's degree in education at Antioch College in Ohio. After her graduate studies, Cotera went to work as a librarian at the Texas State Library in Austin; in 1968, she became director of the Southwest Educational Development Laboratory.

The next year, Cotera and her husband, Juan Estanislao Cotera, helped organize a walkout of Mexican-American students in Crystal City, Texas. Hispanic students were protesting their lack of access to academic programs; their actions also called attention to the absence of Hispanic representation in local government, even though Hispanics constituted more than 90 percent of the city's population at the time.

After the walkout, Cotera became involved in the creation of the **Texas Women's Political Caucus**, and with the Chicano movement's newly formed **La Raza Unida Party** (LRUP). In 1972, she ran unsuccessfully as the LRUP's candidate for the Texas State Board of Education. In 1974, she founded the nonprofit **Chicana Research and Learning Center** in Austin. It provides research, information, and funding for projects, primarily for those by minority women.

Cotera has written and published several books and resources that reflect her experience as an educator and as an activist for Hispanics, and Hispanic women in particular. In the 1960s, she and her husband published the *Educator's Guide to Chicano Resources*. She published *Chicanas in Politics and Public Life* in 1975, and *Dona Doormat No Esta Aqui: An Assertiveness and Communications Skills Manual for Hispanic Women* in 1984.

Cotera has also written several essays, such as "The Women Say/The Men Say: Women's Liberation and Men's Consciousness," and "Twice a Minority: Mexican-American Women." In 1976, she published "Profile of the Mexican-American Woman," a highly regarded historical resource.

Cotera started her own company in 1975, **Information Systems Development,** which published the bilingual "Austin Hispanic Directory" and other resources. In 1980, she co-founded **Mexican-American Business and Professional Women** in Austin, a political organization to empower Latina women. Cotera is also a teacher of American History at Austin Community College.

Martha Cotera

Carolina Herrera
(1939–)

Fashion designer to the rich and famous, **Carolina Herrera** did not embark on her profession in a typical manner. A wealthy socialite and the mother of four children, she began her career after she turned 40, because she wanted to "try something new."

Maria Carolina Josefina Pacanins y Nino was born in Caracas, Venezuela. Her father was a military officer and a government official. Her upbringing in a prominent family exposed her to a social life in high society—including parties, meeting important people, glamour, and fashion. As a little girl, she designed dresses for her dolls; as a young woman, she designed them for herself and her friends. She married the son of a wealthy matriarch in 1969, which exposed her to even greater luxury and expanded her opportunities to dress fashionably.

When Herrera unveiled her first line of clothes in 1981, fashion experts were skeptical. Many saw her as a well-dressed socialite who would never be taken seriously as a designer. However, her creations surprised everyone. They reflected her sophistication and talent, and she was widely praised within the industry. Herrera's designs combined provocative, plunging necklines and exaggerated "fairy-tale shoulders," with a look of taste and flair. Her expertise quickly made her a popular designer, with clients from an international elite that included royalty, political wives, and movie stars.

Throughout the 1980s, Herrera displayed her versatility and her ability to adopt to changing tastes, as she designed outfits that were much less exaggerated than her previous creations. Her own version of the new slim style was a trendsetter for the decade. During that time, former First Lady, and an American fashion trendsetter herself, **Jacqueline Kennedy Onassis** paid Herrera the ultimate compliment when she asked her

Carolina Herrera

to design the wedding dress for her daughter, **Caroline Kennedy**. In 1987, Herrera received another great honor, when **Hispanic Designers, Inc.**, voted her the award as the **Top Hispanic Designer**.

In 1988, Herrera ventured into another arena, when she introduced her own line of perfume. The popular Carolina Herrera perfume combines the odors of jasmine and tuberose, which for the designer conjure up images of a happy childhood in Venezuela.

Herrera continued to design during the 1980s and '90s, creating new styles and impressing the fashion world with her creativity. Versatile and imaginative, all of her designs have reflected her elegant style as well as her sense of function, to coincide with her belief that designs must remain realistic to be marketable. "No one wants to look like a costume," she has said.

Herrera has divided both her professional and personal life with homes in New York City and Caracas.

Lee Trevino
(1939–)

After he won his first **U.S. Open** golf championship, **Lee Trevino** joked that he would use his prize money to "buy the Alamo and give it back to Mexico." One of the greatest and most personable players in golf history, Lee Trevino, helped break down the racial and class barriers that had long made golf an exclusive game for wealthy white people.

Born near Dallas, Texas, Trevino grew up in poverty. His mother was a maid, and his grandfather, who helped raise him, worked as a gravedigger. They lived in a shack that had no electricity or running water.

Lee Trevino

The home was adjacent to a golf course, and as a boy, Trevino collected stray balls and sold them to golfers for pocket change. When his uncle gave him an old club and some used balls, he started teaching himself to play. Sometimes he sneaked onto the country club golf course to play a few holes. Other times, he practiced on a makeshift course in his backyard.

Trevino left school after the seventh grade to work and help support his family. He took a job on a golf course as a caddy and a greens keeper, which gave him the opportunity to practice and refine his skills. His favorite ploy was to challenge the country club members with a makeshift club he built. To their surprise, he usually won.

Trevino spent a few years in the U.S. Marines, where he continued to improve his golf game. He then settled in El Paso, Texas, where he became a country club pro, giving lessons to members. He soon joined the professional golfing tour, and before long, became a major contender. In 1967, he was named Rookie of the Year after he finished fifth at the U.S. Open. The next year, he won the Open.

For the next 18 years, Trevino was one of the most dominating players on the tour, with earnings of more than $3 million. For 14 of those years, he had a streak of at least one major tournament victory every year. He won the U.S. Open again in 1971. He also won the **British Open** twice and the **Canadian Open** three times. He became a crowd favorite for his wisecracking yet friendly demeanor. His fans, nicknamed "Lee's Fleas," called him "Super Mex."

In 1975, Trevino and two other golfers were struck by lightning. They all survived, but not without sustaining injury. As a result of the accident, Trevino suffered from severe back pain that plagued him throughout the rest of his career.

Trevino never forgot his hard times growing up. During his career, he donated much of his earnings to charitable organizations.

66. Vicki Carr
(1940–)

Few female vocalists have had as much success as a crossover artist as **Vicki Carr**. Born Florencia Bicenta de Casillas Martinez Cardona in El Paso, Texas, Carr was the eldest of seven children. Her love of music showed itself early, when she sang in a Christmas play at the age of four.

After her birth, the family moved to Rosemead, California where Carr was raised. The move brought her closer to Los Angeles, which aided the start of her professional career.

Carr took her first professional singing job after high school as the vocalist for Pepe Callahan's Mexican-Irish Band. Shortly after that, she went solo. Calling herself "Carlita," she performed in nightclubs and had her first headline engagement at the famous **Coconut Grove**.

Carr signed her first recording contract in 1961 with **Liberty Records** and had two top 40 hits, although not in the United States. "He's a Rebel" was an Australian hit. "It Must Be Him" reached number three on the charts in England. Years later, the song was featured in the hit movie *Moonstruck*.

In the late 1960s, Carr set new standards for sold-out concerts in countries all across Europe—Germany, Spain, France, England, Holland—and in Australia and Japan. In 1967, she played a command performance for England's Queen Elizabeth II. By the 1970s, Carr had returned to the United States, signed a contract with **Columbia Records**, and began to appear on television variety shows.

Although a hit with her English-language pop music, Carr didn't forget her heritage. In the 1970s, she showed her versatility by crossing over into Spanish-language songs. The move brought her additional international fame.

Carr had her first performance in Mexico in 1972, and has been a star there ever since. She released her first Spanish-language album, "Vikki Carr, En Espanol," in the same year. Two other Spanish-language albums, "Cosas del Amor" and "Esos Hombres," went gold throughout Latin America and the United States. Her 1985 album, "Simplemente Mujer", won a **Grammy** for Spanish-language album. By the end of the 1990s, Carr had produced 50 best-selling albums, including 17 gold records.

Being a crossover artist has presented some challenges. When Carr changed her stage name from Carlita to Vikki Carr, her father protested. She confidently reassured him, "I will be as well known as a Mexican-American as an Anglo." During her lengthy career, Carr has also joined with another successful crossover artist, **Linda Rondstadt** (see no. 79), performing concerts with mariachi bands.

Vicki Carr

Luis Valdez was born in Delano, California. Like many children of migrant workers, he and his nine brothers and sisters attended several different schools as his parents traveled up and down the Central Valley taking seasonal farm work.

Eventually, the family settled in San Jose, California, and Valdez earned a scholarship in 1960 to attend college there. While at California State University, San Jose, he first revealed his promising talents as a playwright. In 1961, his one-act play, *The Theft*, won a writing contest. Two years later, the school's drama department produced his first full-length play, *The Shrunken Head of Pancho Villa*.

Valdez earned his bachelor's degree in 1964, then moved north to join the theatrical group, the **San Francisco Mime Troupe**. It was there that he learned the dramatic device known as **agitprop** (agitation and propaganda) theater, which he incorporated into his future work.

In 1965, Valdez returned to Delano to join **César Chávez** (see no. 47) and the farmworkers' movement. Valdez tapped into his theatrical background, especially the agitprop theater, to form a troupe for farmworkers. **El Teatro Campesino** toured the migrant camps performing *actos* (one-act plays) that explored the political and cultural issues of the movement.

In the 1970s, Chicano theater blossomed into a full-blown national movement, largely pioneered by Valdez and El Teatro Campesino. Chicano theater adhered to Valdez's belief that theaters should remain true to *la raza* (the Mexican people). In 1978, Valdez wrote, directed, and produced the play *Zoot Suit*, which was based on the 1940s **Zoot Suit riots** in Los Angeles. It was a hit in Los Angeles theaters, and eventually went on to have a successful run on Broadway in New York City. It was the first play written and produced by a Mexican-American to ever be performed there.

While the Chicano theater movement dissipated in the 1980s, in a brief period it had created an entirely new art form that incorporated Mexican theatrical traditions as well as increasing national awareness of Hispanic social issues.

From theater Valdez turned to the medium of film, and it was here that Valdez achieved his greatest success. In 1982, he directed the film adaptation of *Zoot Suit*, and in 1987, he directed the hit movie *La Bamba*, which told the story of the Hispanic rock-'n'-roll star **Richie Valens**. Valdez continued his work in stage and film throughout the next decade and into the 21st century.

The pioneering work of Valdez, the "**father of Chicano theater**," has helped create countless opportunities for Hispanic artists and increased understanding of Hispanic issues in the United States.

Luis Valdez

As a novelist and screenwriter, **Victor Villaseñor** has chronicled the difficult experiences of the millions of Mexicans who have immigrated to the United States. He is a self-taught writer who has helped introduce **Chicano literature** into the American mainstream.

Born in Carlsbad, California to Mexican immigrant parents, Villaseñor struggled in school as a boy. He spoke Spanish as his primary language, and his difficulties were compounded by dyslexia, a learning disability. He dropped out of high school and went to work in the fields on the ranch where his father worked. Later, he earned his income as a construction worker. He tried college in San Diego, but again had difficulty and dropped out of school altogether.

Villaseñor then took a trip to Mexico that changed his life. His discovered his heritage there, as well as a love for literature. He returned to the United States with a newfound passion for reading and writing. He read voraciously and taught himself how to write fiction. In his time off from construction work, he wrote a total of 9 novels and 65 short stories over a period of ten years. Unfortunately, all of them were rejected for publication.

Villaseñor had received more than 200 rejections when, in 1973, Bantam Books accepted his novel, *Macho!*, for publication. The novel, which received critical acclaim, tells the painful story of a young Mexican who enters the United States illegally to find work. He returns to his native country with a changed attitude about traditional values, especially the ethic of machismo.

In 1977, Villaseñor turned to nonfiction. He published *Jury: The People versus Juan Corona*, which chronicled the life and trial of a serial killer. In 1983, he ventured into the world of film, when he wrote a screenplay, *The Ballad of Gregorio Cortez*. The successful movie starred well-known Hispanic actor **Edward James Olmos** (see no. 81).

Meanwhile, Villaseñor was researching his next book. *Rain of Gold*, which was released in 1992, told the multi-generational saga of his own family. It included the family's history in Mexico, as well as in the United States. For the book, he conducted extensive interviews with family members, and he used traditional elements of Mexican folktales and the oral tradition to tell the story. It was a national bestseller, and he followed it in 1996 with a sequel, entitled *Wild Steps of Heaven*.

Victor Villaseñor

In addition to writing, Villaseñor is a popular speaker on a variety of topics, including family, pride, and world peace—an issue he has adopted as his personal project. In 1992, he conducted his first annual "Snow Goose Global Thanksgiving for World-Wide Peace."

Joan Báez

Born to a Mexican father and a British mother in Staten Island, New York, **Joan Báez** became one of America's most successful pop-folk singers and an outspoken political activist.

Báez's father was a physicist and her mother was a drama teacher. She lived in a number of college towns around the country as her parents pursued their professional careers.

Báez took up music at a young age, singing in her high school choir. With her distinctively ethereal soprano voice, she was designated as a soloist with star potential and began signing professionally at the age of 18. She gained wide attention with her performance at the 1959 **Newport Folk Festival** in Rhode Island.

The following year, Báez released her debut album, entitled simply, "Joan Báez." Each of her first three albums went gold and stayed on the bestseller charts for more than two years. Overall, she has recorded eight gold albums in a career that has spanned more than 40 years.

Báez reached star status during the 1960s, when the country was confronting a number of powerful social issues. These issues had a profound effect on her, and she became not only one of the most popular folk singers in the country, but an icon of **social activism**. In the early 60s, she used her growing popularity in the music business to help sponsor an up-and-coming young folksinger named **Bob Dylan**. The two became close friends and performed together several times over the course of their careers.

Over the years, Báez has become associated with a number of causes. She became a strong advocate for Hispanic farmworkers in California. She worked closely with **César Chavez** (see no. 47), helping him raise money. *Time* magazine ran a feature story on her in 1962 for her efforts to racially desegregate the southern college campuses. During the 1960s, she also became an outspoken critic of the America's involvement in the **Vietnam War**, which earned her scorn from conservatives and other supporters of the war around the country. However, after the war ended, she wrote an "Open Letter to the Socialist Republic of Vietnam," protesting the policies of the new communist government.

Báez has founded two organizations: the **Institute for the Study of Nonviolence** (1965) and the **Humanitas International Human Rights Committee** (1979). She also helped found **Amnesty West Coast**, a branch of the human-rights organization Amnesty International. In 1968, Báez married fellow social activist David Harris; the marriage lasted until 1973.

Báez continued her work on behalf of social causes into the 1980s, when most of her fellow activists had retired to more comfortable lives. She has written two books: *Daybreak* (1968) and *A Voice to Sing With: A Memoir* (1986).

Lucille Roybal-Allard
(1941-)

The first Mexican-American woman to serve in the United States Congress, **Lucille Roybal-Allard** originally had no desire to enter into politics.

Born and raised in the Boyle Heights community of Los Angeles, a predominantly Mexican-American neighborhood, Roybal-Allard became active at an early age in political campaigns for her father, Congressman **Ed Roybal** (see no. 35). Her mother was her father's campaign manager, running his headquarters out of their home, and the children helped by folding letters, stuffing envelopes, and licking stamps. When she was older, Roybal-Allard walked precincts and helped register voters.

However, she didn't like the lack of privacy that came with political celebrity. So, after earning her bachelor's degree from California State University, Los Angeles in 1961, she chose another line of work. Roybal-Allard served as the executive director of the **National Association of Hispanic CPAs**, in Washington D.C. From there, she became the assistant director for the Alcoholism Council of East Los Angeles; later, she worked as a planning associate for the United Way.

In 1987, Roybal-Allard's altered her outlook on politics. She had grown frustrated by her inability to effect change in the community, and, with her children grown, she decided to run for a vacant local **California Assembly** seat. In a field of nine candidates, she won the election handily.

Roybal-Allard had a noticeable impact in the Assembly. Emphasizing empowerment of the community, she helped organize a local group of women, the **Mothers of East L.A.**, which assisted her in a protracted fight to defeat a proposal to build a prison in the district. Capitalizing on the grass-roots support she helped organize, she also worked to defeat a proposal to build a toxic incinerator in the

neighborhood. Later, she authored a bill that requires an environmental impact report to be issued for any proposed toxic incinerator in California.

Roybal-Allard has also fought successfully to protect the rights of women. She authored several bills that give greater protection to victims of domestic abuse, rape, and sexual misconduct. The National Organization for Women (NOW) named her "**Legislator of the Year**" in 1991.

Lucille Roybal-Allard

The following year, Roybal-Allard took the big step of filling her father's shoes. When Ed Roybal retired from Congress in 1992, she won the election to replace him as the representative for California's 33rd District. In Congress, she has worked to continue her father's legacy, in addition to focusing on the issues that were important to her in the California Assembly. Among other things, she has sponsored legislation to increase education regarding the citizenship process for immigrants and refugees.

Clarissa Pinkola Estés
(1943–)

Clarissa Pinkola Estés was born in Mexico to mestizo parents—Mexicans of European and American Indian descent—but she was raised by her adoptive Hungarian immigrant parents in the state of Michigan. Her exposure to various ethnic cultures in her upbringing played an important part in her development as a pioneering psychologist and writer.

Clarissa Pinkola Estés

Estés was raised in a wooded region near the Great Lakes. She lived in a racially mixed community, with Eastern Europeans, Mexicans, Puerto Ricans, African-Americans, and American southerners. Growing up she was greatly influenced by the stories she was told by her Hungarian aunts. During her childhood, she also developed a love for the outdoors, and especially for wolves, which are prominent in the woods of the northern Midwest.

When Estés was in her thirties, she located her natural parents. By reconnecting with her natural family, she discovered the folklore and customs of her Mexican ancestry. This, too, influenced her writing because, as she says,

"people who are twice born as adoptees, especially if they are adopted into another culture, have the special ability to bridge those groups."

In 1976, Estés received her bachelor's degree in psychotherapeutics from Denver's Loretto Heights College. In 1981, she earned her Ph.D. in **ethno-clinical psychology**—the psychology of ethnic groups, especially tribes—from the Union Institute in Cincinnati, Ohio. In 1984, she earned her post-doctoral diploma in analytical psychology from the Inter-Regional Society of Jungian Analysts in Zurich, Switzerland. Jungian analysis, named after the psychologist **Carl Jung**, uses storytelling to explore a person's subconscious.

As a specialist in **cross-cultural mythology**, Estés used the Jungian technique to develop a new psychology for women. She combines storytelling and dream analysis to help patients uncover issues in their subconscious and heal their psychological wounds.

Estés has created audio tapes and has published poetry, but her most notable achievement came in 1992, with the publication of her book *Women Who Run With the Wolves: Myths and Stories of the Wild Woman Archetype*. Based on 20 years of research, the book includes numerous stories from various ethnic groups. Through these stories Estés establishes a link between women's natural characteristics and instincts and those of wolves. She uses the link to teach women to trust their instincts and tap into their "wild woman selves." The book was a huge success, appearing on the *New York Times* bestseller list only five weeks after it was published.

Estés is a married mother of three daughters. She is an artist in residence for the state of Colorado. She also practices psychoanalysis in Colorado and Wyoming.

72. Vilma Martínez
(1943–)

A leader in the Hispanic **civil rights** movement, **Vilma Socorro Martínez**, experienced first-hand the psychological damage of discrimination and stereotypes as a young girl growing up in Texas.

Martínez was born in San Antonio. Her grandmother taught her to read and write in Spanish before she went to school. When she entered the first grade, she had no fear of learning English.

Although Martínez was an honor student in junior high school, her guidance counselor tried to convince her to attend a vocational high school because she was of Mexican descent. She ignored the advice and attended an academic school, where she excelled. When she neared graduation, she had a similar experience. Her counselor refused to help her apply for college, so she did it herself.

While in high school, Martínez worked one summer for a friend of her father who was a well-known lawyer and civil rights activist. The experience convinced her that she wanted to become a lawyer. She attended the University of Texas at Austin with the help of an academic scholarship, and completed her studies in only two and a half years. In 1964, she enrolled at Columbia University Law School, again with the help of scholarships, and she received her law degree in 1967.

After law school, Martínez took a job with the Legal Defense Fund of the National

Vilma Martínez

Association for the Advancement of Colored People (NAACP). In the early 1970s, she became involved in an effort to form a Chicano civil rights group, the **Mexican-American Legal Defense and Educational Fund** (MALDEF). In 1973, she was elected president and chief legal counsel of the new organization.

As president, Martínez helped turn MALDEF into a powerful force in the civil rights movement. Under her leadership, the organization scored several major legal victories. It sued and won the right for Spanish-speaking children to have bilingual classes in public schools. It won a lawsuit against the Texas State Legislature, a ruling that stated that the "at large" election process deprived minorities of adequate political representation. MALDEF also succeeded in bringing Mexican-Americans under the protection of the national **Voting Rights Act**. Martínez's tenure as president lasted for nine years.

Martínez later went into private law practice in Los Angeles, but she remained on the MALDEF board of directors, and she became involved in a number of other public service organizations. She served for 14 years, two as chairperson, on the University of California Board of Regents. She was also a member of the board of the **Southwest Voter Registration and Education Project** (SVREP) in the 1980s.

Controversial as well as a pioneer, **Geraldo Rivera** is best known for his shocking talk shows and his sensational style of television journalism. However, he has also been a highly regarded investigative reporter who has won numerous industry awards for his work.

Rivera was born in New York City to a Puerto Rican father and a Jewish mother. He was conflicted over his mixed ethnic background and changed his name briefly to Jerry Rivers to avoid discrimination. He eventually came to accept and embrace both of his heritages and reclaimed his given name.

After high school, Rivera joined the merchant marines. He earned his bachelor's degree from the University of Arizona in 1965 and his law degree from the Brooklyn Law School in 1969. He then became a practicing attorney in New York City. He worked as a poverty lawyer and became the spokesman for a radical Puerto Rican movement, the **Young Lords**.

Rivera's work for the group caught the attention of WABC-TV, a local television station seeking to recruit minority broadcasters. He was hired to work as a newscaster, and quickly established himself as an aggressive investigative reporter.

Rivera's breakthrough story, "Drug Crisis in East Harlem," earned him the New York State Associated Press Broadcasters Association Award in 1971. In 1972, he profiled the deplorable conditions at the **Willowbrook State School for the Mentally Retarded** on Staten Island. The story earned him a job as host of the national program "Good Night, America." Later, he also went to work as a reporter for "Good Morning, America." In 1978, he became a special correspondent for the ABC news magazine "20/20." He held that job for seven years and continued to build his reputation as a sensationalist journalist.

In 1985, Rivera's much-anticipated program, "The Opening of Al Capone's Vault," was a major disappointment when the opened vault revealed nothing more than old glass bottles. In 1987, he debuted his own show, "Geraldo," which transformed the previously tame daytime talk show format by featuring shocking guests and controversial topics. On an episode about teenage white supremacists, a brawl broke out and Rivera suffered a broken nose in the scuffle.

Rivera has had a troubled personal life. His first two marriages ended in divorce. He has been ridiculed for being self-indulgent and insincere about his love for his Latino heritage. However, he has also won the respect of his peers by receiving numerous awards, including seven Emmys, three Broadcasters of the Year, and a Peabody.

In 1994, he debuted an issues-oriented news program, "Rivera Live," on CNBC. In late 2001, Rivera announced he was leaving the program to resume his career as a reporter to cover the U.S. war in Afghanistan.

Geraldo Rivera

One of the most influential Hispanic activists of the 20th century, **William Cárdenas Velásquez**, was born in San Antonio, Texas. He became involved in politics as a teenager, when he worked on his uncle's campaign for the local school board.

In 1966, Velásquez earned his bachelor's degree in economics from St. Mary's University in San Antonio. He went on to study for his master's degree in economics, but by this time he had become a full-time activist. He left the program just before completing his degree and went to work with **César Chávez** (see no. 47), who at the time was organizing farmworkers in Texas.

Later, Velásquez joined the staff of the **Mexican-American Legal Defense and Education Fund** (MALDEF). Then he went to work for the Southwest Council of La Raza, which later became the **National Council of La Raza.** Soon, he became convinced that the greatest tool for Hispanic empowerment in the United States was greater participation in the electoral process. To achieve that end, he founded the **Southwest Voter Registration Education Project** (SVREP) in 1974. He became the group's executive director and retained that post for 14 years.

William C. Velásquez

The SVREP employed several tactics that distinguished it from other Hispanic civil rights groups. First, it operated on a grassroots, community level that included local volunteer recruitment, training, and coalition building. It also focused on encouraging more Hispanics to vote and run for elected office. In addition, the organization conducted research of voting patterns in the Hispanic community, which provided powerful evidence in lawsuits against unfairly drawn electoral districts.

The SVREP was tremendously successful under Velásquez's leadership. Over the years, the organization conducted hundreds of voter registration drives in more than a dozen states. It won more than 80 lawsuits challenging election districts that denied Hispanics their political influence. Most importantly, Hispanic voter registration throughout the United States rose from three million to five million, and the number of Hispanics in elected positions doubled. Many of the increases took place in Texas, where the organization was headquartered. Gradually the SVREP expanded into California and other areas where the election process was not providing proper representation to the Hispanic population.

Velásquez received national notoriety for his accomplishments. Some people have called him the single most important organizer of Hispanics to political power. In the early 1980s, he lectured at the Institute of Politics at Harvard University's John F. Kennedy School of Public Affairs. In 1988, Massachusetts Governor **Michael Dukakis** asked him to serve in his campaign for the Democratic party's presidential nomination. Velásquez accepted the invitation, but he died from cancer a short time later.

José Angel Gutiérrez
(1944–)

José Angel Gutiérrez

One of the most influential leaders of the Chicano movement in the 1960s and 70s, **José Angel Gutiérrez** was born in Crystal City, Texas into the family of an affluent doctor. However, his father died when he was 12 years old, and the family was forced to earn a living by working in the fields.

Gutiérrez was a bright student who was elected student body president of his predominantly white high school. He earned his B.A. in political science from Texas Arts and Industries University in 1966. In 1968, he earned a master's degree in the same field from St. Mary's University in San Antonio. He got his Ph.D. in political science from the University of Texas at Austin in 1976, and later obtained a law degree from the University of Houston.

In 1967, Gutiérrez and several other St. Mary's students founded a local chapter of the **Mexican-American Youth Organization,** which lobbied for improvements in Hispanic educational opportunities and for other causes.

In 1969, he aided the Crystal City student walk-out, which protested discriminatory practices at the local high school. The event prompted him to co-found the **La Raza Unida Party** (LRUP, the United People Party) to address the political disenfranchisement of Chicanos in the community. Although Mexican-Americans comprised more than 80 percent of the small town's population, whites held all the local political power.

In 1970, Gutiérrez and two other LRUP candidates were elected to the Crystal City School Board. Gutiérrez later became chairperson of the board. The shift in the balance of power resulted in a number of changes, including the creation of bilingual education programs.

In 1972, Gutiérrez was elected president of the national LRUP in a closely fought campaign against another high-profile activist, **"Corky" Gonzales** (see no. 52). The election symbolized a victory for Gutiérrez's more moderate policies. He advocated working within the existing two-party system, rather than forming a national third party.

In 1974, Gutiérrez was elected judge in Zavala County, Texas. The next year, he accepted an invitation from **Fidel Castro** to visit Cuba. The visit, combined with his long history of activism, strained his relations with the white members of the legal establishment, and he eventually resigned his judgeship. He moved to Oregon and became a college professor, but he returned to Texas in 1986 as the director of the **Greater Dallas Legal and Community Development Foundation**, a nonprofit advocacy group for the poor.

In 1990, Gutiérrez became an administrative law judge for the city of Dallas. In the early 1990s, he ran an unsuccessful campaign for the U.S. Senate in Texas. For the rest of the decade, Gutiérrez continued to operate the **José Angel Gutiérrez Legal Center**.

A native of Puerto Rico, **Antonia Novello** dedicated herself to helping people who suffer from poor health after her own childhood experience with illness. She translated that commitment into a lifelong career in medicine and public health, which culminated in her appointment as the **Surgeon General** of the United States.

Novello was born in Fajardo, Puerto Rico, where she and her brother were raised by their divorced mother. As a young girl, Novello suffered from a painful congenital colon condition, which was not corrected until she was 18. The experience gave her a desire to help other people who suffered from health problems.

After earning her M.D. from the University of Puerto Rico School of Medicine in 1970, Novello moved to Michigan. She studied nephrology at the University of Michigan Medical Center. After completing a fellowship there and another at Georgetown University, she worked in private practice as a pediatrician in Springfield, Virginia.

In 1978, Novello joined the **Public Health Service Commissioned Corps**. During this time, she developed an interest in children with AIDS, and she earned an M.P.H. (Master's in Public Health) from the John Hopkins School of Hygiene and Public Health. She also worked as a consultant to the U. S. Senate Committee on Labor and Human Resources, and was involved in the drafting and enactment of legislation on organ transplants and cigarette warning labels. Over the next several years, Novello climbed the ranks of the **National Institute of Health** (NIH), becoming the deputy director of the National Institute of Child Health and Human Development (NICHD) by 1986.

In 1990, President **George Bush** appointed Novello Surgeon General of the United States after the retirement of **C. Everett Koop**. She was the first Hispanic and the first woman to hold the post, and she faced high expectations based on the tenure of her popular and outspoken predecessor. Her appointment was also controversial because of her opposition to abortion.

Antonia Novello

Novello soon established her own identity and silenced her critics. Her tenure as surgeon general was noted for its emphasis on a number of important children's and women's health issues, such as AIDS prevention, immunization, and underage drinking and smoking. Most notably, she spoke out strongly against the slick marketing of tobacco and alcohol products to teenagers.

Novello held the post of surgeon general until 1993. She then served as the United Nations Children's Fund (UNICEF) Special Representative for Health and Nutrition, and she returned to teaching at Johns Hopkins University. She was appointed Commissioner of Health for the State of New York in 1999.

Richard Rodriguez
(1944–)

Born in San Francisco, the third of four children, **Richard Rodriguez** was raised in Sacramento by hard-working parents who were, in his words, "nobody's victims." Until he was five years-old, the family spoke only Spanish in the home. He knew a little English, just enough to run errands for his mother at neighborhood stores.

Richard Rodriguez

When his parents enrolled him in the local Catholic school, Rodriguez struggled. Some of the nuns from the school visited the Rodriguez home and insisted that he practice English there. His parents complied. The results were soon apparent. He began to feel like an American. He succeeded in school, and he became an avid reader. He became a star student and earned an academic scholarship to Stanford University.

Rodriguez earned his bachelor's degree in English from Stanford in 1967 and a master's degree in philosophy from Columbia University in 1969. Then he enrolled in the Ph.D. program in English at the University of California at Berkeley.

In 1974, while a student at Berkeley, Rodriguez was awarded a **Fulbright Fellowship,** which he used to study at the Warburg Institute in London, where he researched his dissertation on Renaissance literature. He returned to Berkeley and, as he neared completion of his Ph.D. studies, began to get offers from prestigious universities to join their faculty.

The offers troubled him. He believed the universities were recruiting him over other candidates who were equally, if not more, qualified simply because he was Hispanic. In protest, he wrote the schools and asked to be removed from consideration.

For many years, Rodriguez worked odd jobs as a janitor or free-lance writer to earn a living. Then in 1981, he published a memoir, *Hunger of Memory: The Education of Richard Rodriguez,* which received critical acclaim. In the book, he attacks bilingual education and affirmative action, two social programs that had assisted countless Hispanic-Americans and other ethnic minorities to overcome discrimination and economic hardship in the United States. The book was extremely controversial, but it was praised for its literary quality.

Ten years later, Rodriguez published a second memoir, *Days of Obligation: An Argument with My Mexican Father,* which addresses his identification with Mexican culture and the loss he felt after assimilating into mainstream America. He also reveals his homosexuality, and he discusses the friends he has lost to AIDS. It was also a critical success.

Beginning in the 1990s, Rodriguez worked as a journalist and essayist for a variety of news organizations, including PBS's "The Jim Lehrer News Hour," and the *Los Angeles Times.*

In 2002, Rodriguez published a third memoir—*Brown, The Last Discovery of America.* In a series of essays, he touches once more on such subjects as what it means to be a Hispanic in America, his relationship with his father, and his hopes for a country where boundaries of race and class no longer exist.

America's foremost muralist, **Judith Baca** has carried on the great Mexican tradition of **mural painting** in the United States, and she has extended her work to a world-wide audience.

Born and raised in South Central Los Angeles, Judith Francisca Baca did not know her father. She was raised by her grandmother while her mother worked in a tire factory. When she was six, her mother married and moved to the city of Pacoima. She was lonely in her new school because she did not speak English well, so she turned to art.

After high school, Baca earned her bachelor's degree, and later her master's, both in art, from California State University, Northridge. She took a job as an art teacher at her alma mater, Bishop Alemany High School, in 1969. While teaching at the Catholic school, Baca and several other teachers and nuns were fired for their protests against the Vietnam War, in an incident known as the "Alemany Eighteen."

Baca took a job with the City of Los Angeles's **Cultural Affairs Division,** and she formed her own group, **Las Vistas Nuevas,** which consisted of several young people from local gangs. Remarkably, she inspired the troubled youths to cooperate, and they helped her paint her first mural in Hollenbeck Park.

In the mid-1970's, Baca traveled to Mexico to study the tradition of Mexican mural painting. She enrolled in classes at the studio of **David Alfaro Siqueiros**, one of Los Tres Grandes (the Three Greats), which also included **Diego Rivera** and **José Clemente Orozco**. She studied their techniques and returned to the United States to carry on the tradition.

Back in Los Angeles, Baca expanded her program, supervising the painting of more than 250 murals. Then she embarked on a project known as the "**Great Wall**." The remarkable mural, which stretches a half-mile along a drainage canal, traces the multi-ethnic history of Los Angeles from prehistoric times to the 1950s.

In 1976, Baca formed the **Social and Public Art Resource Center** (SPARC) in Venice, California. The nonprofit art center works to preserve murals and other public art.

In 1987, Baca launched an even bigger project. "**World Wall: A Vision of the Future Without Fear**" is a huge, multi-panel display, painted by Baca and other international artists. The first four panels of the project were unveiled in Finland in June, 1990. Then it traveled to Gorky Park in the Soviet Union. Baca envisioned the portable mural as "a world-wide collaborative" that focuses on war, peace, and international cooperation.

Baca later became a full professor of art at the University of California at Irvine.

Judith Baca

Linda Ronstadt was born with a nonconforming spirit. Her rebelliousness fed an inventive music career that has embraced numerous styles and lasted several decades.

She was born into a musical family in Tucson, Arizona. Her grandfather, **Federico Ronstadt**, emigrated from Mexico to Tucson in 1882. He organized a popular musical group there, in addition to a successful carriage business. His daughter, Luisa, became the internationally known Hispanic folk singer and actress **Luisa Espinel.** Linda's father was not a professional musician; he owned a hardware store in Tucson. However, he loved to sing and play Mexican music with his daughter, who at the age of six, decided she wanted to become a singer.

At the age of 18, Ronstadt dropped out of the University of Arizona to sing with her boyfriend's band, the **Stone Poneys**, in Los Angeles. The band was moderately successful, opening for The Doors on a concert tour, and releasing a hit single, "Different Drum," in 1967. However, in the same year, the band broke up and Ronstadt was on her own.

She embarked on a solo career, releasing her first two albums, "Hand Sown...Home Grown" and "Silk Purse," in 1969 and 1970. Both albums were some of the first to successfully blend country music with rock'n' roll.

Linda Ronstadt

Ronstadt's early years as a professional musician were not without difficulty. She battled a stressful concert schedule, drug problems, troubled romances, and a bad case of stage fright. Eventually, she conquered her demons and went on to become the premiere female rock star of the 1970s. She had a series of platinum (million-selling) albums. Many of her hits, such as "When Will I Be Loved?," "Blue Bayou," and "Poor, Poor Pitiful Me," became the signature songs of a generation.

Ronstadt is also a gifted soprano. In 1981, she surprised critics and fans with her performance of Mable in the Broadway opera production of *The Pirates of Penzance*. Few performers have successfully transitioned from rock'n'roll to opera, but Ronstadt accomplished it.

In the mid-1980s, Ronstadt made yet another daring crossover with the release of three albums of vintage torch songs, "What's New," "Lush Life," and "For Sentimental Reasons." During the 1980s, Ronstadt also called attention to herself outside of the musical arena when she became temporarily romantically involved with **Jerry Brown**, then governor of California.

In the late 1980s and early 1990s, Ronstadt returned to her roots with the release of two albums featuring her father's favorite mariachi songs. The albums were popular with critics and fans, and they further demonstrated her seemingly limitless musical versatility.

Henry Cisneros
(1947–)

Born and raised in **San Antonio**, Texas, **Henry Cisneros** was struck with a passion for public service. He attended Catholic school in his hometown, and in 1964, he enrolled at Texas A&M University. He received his bachelor's degree in 1968, and immediately took a job in the public policy arena.

Cisneros went to work as an analyst for the Lyndon B. Johnson Model Cities Program for Urban Revitalization. In 1970, he became an administrative assistant to the executive vice president of the **National League of Cities**. The following year, he took a job as a White House Fellow.

In the early 1970s, Cisneros enrolled in the master's program in public administration at Harvard University, specializing in urban and regional planning. He earned his degree in 1974, and a few years later, received his Ph.D. from George Washington University. He then returned to his hometown as a faculty member of the University of Texas at San Antonio in the Division of Environmental Studies.

Meanwhile, Cisneros became involved in civic affairs. In 1975, at the age of 27, he became the youngest council member in the history of San Antonio. He was reelected twice, and in 1981, as an independent candidate, he was elected **mayor**. He was the first Mexican-American mayor of San Antonio since **Juan N. Sequín** (see no. 12) in 1842, and the first Hispanic mayor of a major U.S. city. He was reelected three times.

As a council member and mayor, Cisneros was known for being a nonpartisan consensus builder. His policies combined economic development with sensitivity to ethnic issues. His leadership helped revitalize the city and draw greater national attention to the issues of Latinos and the urban poor.

In 1992, President **Bill Clinton** appointed Cisneros **Secretary of Housing and Urban Development**. Cisneros took over a troubled

Henry Cisneros

organization and had to address the pressing problems of homelessness, mortgage discrimination, and fair housing. During his tenure, Cisneros advocated suburban housing projects as a means of reducing the concentration of minorities in inner-city ghettos.

Unfortuantely, Cisneros's service at HUD was tainted by scandal. In 1997, he resigned from the post under pressure stemming from charges that he had lied to the FBI about payoffs he made to a woman with whom he had once been romantically involved. He eventually pleaded guilty to the charge and was fined $10,000. President Clinton pardoned him a few years later.

After stepping down, Cisneros became the president and chief executive officer of the Spanish-language television network **Univision**. In 2000, he founded **American City Vista**, which develops affordable housing within inner and neglected city areas.

Edward James Olmos
(1947–)

Very few people have achieved celebrity status as both an **actor** and a **community activist**, but that is exactly what **Edward James Olmos** has accomplished.

Growing up poor in the East Los Angeles neighborhood of Boyle Heights, Olmos's first love was baseball. He worked so hard at the sport that he became the state batting champion for his age group.

Edward James Olmos

When he was 15, Olmos's love for baseball faded, and he found a new passion in music. Throughout his teenage years, he sang, danced, and played piano for his own rock group, Pacific Ocean, performing at nightclubs on the Sunset Strip in Los Angeles.

Music didn't pay the bills, however, and Olmos was forced to deliver antique furniture during the day for extra income. Meanwhile, he attended college at night. One semester, he took a drama course, to help build his self-confidence for singing. Soon he discovered that he had found yet another interest.

Although Olmos never expected to have a career in acting, he took small acting roles and continued to sing in the evenings, while he worked during the day. Then he got his first big break. In the mid-1970s, he performed the lead role of El Pachuco in **Luis Valdez's** famous play, *Zoot Suit* (see no. 67). Olmos received the Los Angeles Critics Circle Award in 1978, and in 1979, when the play opened on Broadway, he was nominated for the prestigious Tony Award.

Olmos's outstanding stage performance earned him an entrance into movies. Memorable roles in popular films such as *Wolfen* and *Blade Runner* soon followed. He also performed the lead role in the PBS television production of the "The Ballad of Gregorio Cortez".

In the 1980s, Olmos portrayed his most well-known television character, Lieutenant Martin Castillo, in the hit show "Miami Vice." The role earned him an Emmy Award for Best Supporting Actor in 1985. More importantly, it propelled him to higher star status and gave him the clout to choose more of his roles according to his principles.

Olmos is most proud of his role in the movie *Stand and Deliver*. In the 1988 film, he portrayed **Jaime Escalante** (see no. 53), a Bolivian-born math teacher who motivates his high school students to excel at calculus. Olmos received an Academy Award nomination for his performance.

Throughout the 1990s and into the 21st century, Olmos continued to perform in movies that portrayed meaningful Hispanic-American characters. Olmos's conscientious approach to the roles he chooses spills over into his personal activism. He has made time for participation in many charitable causes, and has spoken to countless high schools and charity organizations over the years.

Federico Peña was born and raised in Texas, where family members going back several generations held **public office.** Peña's great-grandfather was the mayor of Laredo during the Civil War, and his grandfather was city alderman there for 25 years.

Peña was an honor student at St. Joseph's Academy in Brownsville. He grew up during the turbulent 1960s, an era of student protests and radical politics, which shaped his liberal political ideology. He attended the University of Texas in Austin, where he earned his Bachelor of Science degree in 1969, and his law degree in 1972.

After law school, Peña went to work in an El Paso legal aid office that offered free legal assistance to poor Hispanics and other minorities. In 1972, he moved to Denver, Colorado and went to work at the **Mexican-American Legal Defense and Educational Fund**. Following that, he worked for the **Chicano Education Project**. Both organizations are prominent advocates for Hispanic civil rights.

In 1979, Peña won a seat in the Colorado General Assembly, where he served for two terms with distinction. He won an award for the Outstanding House Democratic Legislator and was chosen to be the House Minority Speaker.

In 1983, Peña made a bold run for mayor of the city of Denver. In a city where Hispanics made up only 18 percent of the population, he was a long-shot candidate. Although early polls gave him only 3 percent of the vote, he waged an aggressive campaign and won the election. Four years later, he was reelected. During his two terms as mayor, Peña gained national attention for his ability to survive controversy and push through difficult projects, such as a new airport and a new convention center. In 1991, he decided not to seek a third term, even though polls for the first time made him the favorite.

Federico Peña

A year after Peña stepped down as mayor, President **Bill Clinton** appointed him **Secretary of Transportation.** While in Washington, Peña maintained his independent political style by incorporating his own philosophy into his policy decisions. His high-profile actions often offended big business.

In 1994, he ignored staff recommendations and issued a finding that the C/K model pick-up trucks manufactured by General Motors constituted a safety hazard. He also upset the automotive industry by promoting the **Intermodal Surface Transportation Efficiency Act**, which encourages local governments to plan for alternate modes of transportation, such as rail and bicycles.

After leaving the Clinton administration in 1998, Peña accepted a job as managing partner in the Denver office of the investment firm Vestar Capital Partners.

83. Carlos Santana
(1947–)

The man who was the creative inspiration behind the style of music known as **Latin Rock** was born in Autlan de Navarro, a small village in the Mexican state of Jalisco. All of the men in **Carlos Santana's** family, going back to his great-grandfather, were musicians. His father played in a mariachi band. He taught his son the basic theories of music and how to play traditional violin.

Santana was more interested in rock-'n'-roll, and at the age of eight he took up the guitar. His family moved to the Mexican border city of Tijuana when he was 11, and he began playing in nightclubs there.

Santana's family moved to California when he was a teenager, and he attended high school in San Francisco. He learned English and discovered the various musical styles that were thriving in the area at the time. He then formed his own group, the Santana Blues Band, which he later shortened to **Santana**.

Carlos Santana

Within a few years, the group was playing at well-known local clubs. Led by Carlos's blistering yet soulful sound on guitar, they began to make their mark with a unique blend of Afro-Cuban, rock'n'roll, and blues styles. The new sound came to be known as Latin Rock.

In 1969, Santana performed before 500,000 people at the famous music festival at **Woodstock**, New York. The event exposed them to a national audience and propelled them to stardom. They earned their first record contract, which led to a string of hit records.

Between 1969 and 1981, the group recorded several albums, all of which reached gold (half a million sales) or platinum (a million sales) status. Some of the group's most enduring hit songs are "Soul Sacrifice," "Evil Ways," "Oye Como Va," and "Black Magic Woman."

During the 1980s, after changes in the group's personnel, Santana recorded fewer albums, but continued to perform for sold-out audiences around the world. However, by the 1990s, Santana's name had faded from the top ranks of the recording industry. While they were still revered for their classic hits from the 1970s, they were not considered relevant to younger audiences.

Then in 1999, Carlos Santana made a huge comeback as a recording artist when he collaborated with several top-selling artists on the enormously popular album "**Supernatural**." The recording reached number one on the *Billboard* chart and produced a number-one single, "Smooth." It won a total of eight Grammy Awards, including album of the year. As the 21st century dawned, Carlos Santana had reemerged as a top recording artist and performer.

84. Ruben Blades
(1948–)

A multi-talented performer who infuses his political views and a love for his Panamanian heritage into his work, **Ruben Blades** has had a successful career in music and acting.

Blades was born in Panama City, the second of five children. He took up music as a teenager, and he made his first public appearance in 1963, singing vocals in his brother Luis's band, **The Saints**.

In 1964, Blades rejected American music, and stopped singing in English, after United States troops killed 21 Panamanian students and injured hundreds more during riots at Balboa High School. The troops would not allow the Panamanian students to fly their national flag alongside the American flag at the high school, which was located in the American controlled Canal Zone.

Following high school, Blades enrolled at the University of Panama to study law. After he earned his degree, he took a job as an attorney for the Banco Nacional de Panama.

In 1974, Blades moved to the United States to pursue music full-time. Within a year, he joined the band of **Willie Colon**. They collaborated on several albums, the most successful of which was "Siembra"("Planting") in 1977. It featured the hit single "Pedro Navaja," a Latin version of the famous song "Mack the Knife;" at the time, it became the best-selling salsa music single in history.

In 1980, Blades wrote and recorded "Tiburon" ("Shark"), a critical satire of the

Ruben Blades

cold war. It enraged Miami's Cuban-expatriate community, which accused him of sympathizing with Communists.

In 1984, Blades formed his own band, **Seis del Solar** (the Tenement Six), which recorded in Spanish and English. In 1985, he received a **Grammy Award** for his album "Escenas." In 1988, he was awarded another Grammy for the album "Antecedente."

In the mid-1980s, Blades earned his master's degree in international law at Harvard University. He also took up acting. He starred in the English-language film, *Crossover Dreams*, as a Latino boxer turned singing sensation. He received an ACE award for best actor in 1990 for his role in the cable movie, *Dead Man Out,* and he was nominated for an Emmy a year later for his role in the television movie *The Josephine Baker Story.*

In 1991, Blades formed his own political party in Panama, called **Papa Egoro,** or Mother Earth, which adopted a platform of "a new era of clean politics in Panama." Blades wanted the party to "speak for Panamanians not represented by General Manuel Noriega," who was known to be corrupt. (Noriega was later convicted of drug trafficking in the United States and imprisoned.) Blades ran for president of Panama in 1993, but was defeated. He continued to act in movies throughout the remainder of the decade.

Rosemary Casals
(1948–)

Rosemary Casals was more than just a great **tennis player**. She was a pioneer and a rebel who helped make lasting changes to her sport.

Born in San Francisco to poor immigrant parents from El Salvador, Casals was raised by her great aunt and great uncle. He was a former Salvadoran national soccer player, and he encouraged her love of sports. He was her first and only tennis coach.

Rosemary Casals

Casals excelled at tennis from an early age. At 16, she was the top junior and woman's player in northern California. At 17, she was ranked 11th in the nation. She reached the semi-finals of the U.S. Tennis Championships at Forest Hills, losing to Maria Bueno of Brazil, the top-ranked player in the world.

In 1966, Casals reached the quarterfinals in doubles at **Wimbledon** in her first appearance there. In the same year, she and her partner, **Billie Jean King**, won the U.S. hard-court and indoor doubles championships.

Casals also won the U.S. hard-court mixed doubles title with **Ian Crookenden**.

Over the next 20 years, Casals won 11 singles titles and reached the **U.S. Open** singles finals twice. She and King won a total of 56 doubles titles, including 12 majors in 15 years and 7 Wimbledon championships.

Casals achieved her success in spite of handicaps. At 5' 2", she was shorter than all her opponents. Like the great **Pancho Gonzales** (see no. 51), she faced racial and class discrimination from the white, upper class tennis establishment. None of this deterred her. Instead, it fed her competitive, anti-establishment nature, which made her successful not only as a player, but as a trendsetter.

Casals was a colorful player, literally. In addition to her dazzling shots, she impressed the crowd with her brightly colored outfits—a bold protest against the tradition of white only outfits. She was also one of the first players to use a metal racquet.

In 1967, Casals and a number of other players successfully challenged organized tennis to accept professional players at the major tournaments, such as Wimbledon and Forest Hills, which previously had accepted only amateurs.

Several years later, Casals helped form the **Virginia Slims**, a women's professional circuit, which offered more prize money than women had received at tournaments organized by the Unites States Lawn Tennis Association. The new circuit upset the male-dominated USLTA, and it drew more attention to women's tennis.

In 1973, Casals helped form the **World Team Tennis League** and played for several teams over a number of years. In 1978, she underwent knee surgery and gradually reduced her playing time. Casals later went to work in broadcasting as a television commentator for women's' tennis.

Cristina Maria Saralegui grew up in a media savvy family. Her grandfather, publishing tycoon Don Francisco Saralegui, had a powerful influence on her, but her success ultimately comes from her own ambition.

In 1960, to escape Cuba's Communist revolution, Saralegui's family left Havana, where she was born, to settle in Miami, Florida. A few years later, she entered the University of Miami to study **mass communication** and creative writing. While in college, she accepted an internship at the Spanish-language magazine *Vanidades Continental*, which evolved into a position as features editor.

In 1973, Saralegui became an editor at *Cosmopolitan-en-Espanol*. Three years later, she took a job as the entertainment editor at the *Miami Herald* newspaper. In 1977, she landed a job as the editor-in-chief of another Spanish language publication, *Intimidades* magazine. Two years after that, she went back to *Cosmopolitan-en-Espanol*, as the editor-in-chief.

Saralegui's greatest successes did not come in the print media. In 1989, she began her own Spanish-language television talk show, **"El show de Cristina."** Referred to by some as "Oprah con salsa," "The Cristina Show" focused on controversial social issues that had previously been considered taboo by the conservative Spanish-language media.

Saralegui was concerned at first that Hispanics would not want to discuss some of these topics. However, after the first show, she received letters and phone calls from people who divulged secrets that Saralegui said she "would not tell my pastor, my doctor, or my husband." She was then convinced that her audience was in need of just the kind of forum she was providing.

Saralegui also encountered hostility from some Hispanics who felt she was "too white"—she is of light skin and has blonde hair—to represent them. She dismissed the criticism as racist, and emphasized the point that the term Hispanic includes a broad range of peoples.

"El show de Cristina" leaped past these initial hurdles and became one of the top ten Spanish-language programs in the United States. In 1991, it won an Emmy Award.

In that same year, Saralegui also debuted a three-minute daily radio show, "Cristina Opina," and she began publishing her monthly lifestyle magazine, *Cristina la Revista* (*Cristina the Magazine*). A year later, she became the first Hispanic to host daily television programs in two languages when she began hosting an English language version of the "El show de Cristina."

In May, 2001, Saralegui opened a 50,000 - square foot production center in west Miami-Dade County to house her media company, **Cristina Saralegui Enterprises**. Later that year, she announced she would end her 12-year stint as host of "El show de Cristina," at the end of the year to concentrate on developing other projects.

Cristina Saralegui

Oscar Hijuelos
(1951–)

Born and raised in New York City, **Oscar Hijuelos** departs from the themes of many Cuban-American authors. Rather than focus on the political turmoil in Cuba, his writing examines the lives and struggles of immigrants in the United States.

Hijuelos was raised by his immigrant parents. His father was a hotel worker and his mother was a homemaker. He attended public schools, then enrolled at the City College of New York, where he received his bachelor's degree and his master's degree in English and writing.

A 1989 edition of *The Mambo Kings*

The story—which mixes fictional characters with some actual real-life circumstances— concerns the lives of two brothers who move from Havana to New York in the 1950s. They form a successful orchestra and appear with **Desi Arnaz** (see no. 36) on his popular television show, "I Love Lucy." Critics lauded the novel for its exuberance, passion, and lyricism, and it won the **Pulitzer Prize** in 1990. In earning the award, Hijuelos became the first Hispanic-American to receive the honor for a work of fiction.

After college, Hijuelos took a job in the advertising industry. He wrote in his spare time, and a number of his short stories were published in literary magazines. His story "Columbus Discovering America" received an outstanding writer award from Pushcart Press in 1978. The award increased his recognition, which helped him win several writing grants and scholarships.

The money allowed Hijuelos to devote himself full-time to writing. As a result, in 1983, he published his first novel, *Our House in the Last World*, which told the story of a Cuban family living in America during the 1940s. The novel received critical acclaim for its heartwarming and lively portrayal of the family's experiences.

In 1989, Hijuelos published his second novel, *The Mambo Kings Play Songs of Love.*

During the 1990s, Hijuelos published his third and fourth novels. *The Fourteen Sisters of Emilio Montez O'Brien* examines machismo and femininity by focusing on the main character, a young boy, and his relationship with his 14 sisters. Critics praised Hijuelos's ability to capture the deepest emotions permeating such a large family.

Empress of the Splendid Season revolves around the life of Lydia España, a Cuban émigré who works as a cleaning woman in Manhattan. In telling the story of España, and the stories of the secret lives she uncovers in her clients' apartments, Hijuelos tells the story of immigrant life in New York City.

As the 21st century began, Hijuelos continued to live and work in New York City. His stirring novels have brought fresh insight into the experiences of Hispanic-American immigrants living in the United States.

88. Aliza Lifshitz
(1951–)

As an educator, television and radio personality, AIDS specialist, editor, and author, **Aliza Lifshitz** is not a typical physician. Following the examples set by her compassionate parents, Lifshitz has dedicated herself, and her practice, to the betterment of **public health** and **education** for the poor and Hispanic communities.

Lifshitz was born to Mexican Jewish parents, both of whom, she says, were "always committed to helping people." Educated as a young girl in private Jewish schools in Mexico City, Lifshitz eventually came to the United States to complete her medical training. She attended Tulane University and the University of California at San Diego before she entered the profession in southern California as a private practicing physician specializing in internal medicine, clinical pharmacology, and endocrinology.

When Lifshitz opened her daily practice, she to began to offer free and low-cost treatment to low-income and indigent patients in the Hispanic community; later she worked with community-based organizations to expand these services.

During the 1980s, Lifshitz became concerned over the spread of AIDS in the Hispanic community, and in particular, the undocumented segment of it. She became an AIDS activist, devoting about one-third of her practice in Los Angeles to the treatment of patients who have tested positive for the HIV virus. Lifshitz became one of the first Latina physicians to get involved in the treatment of AIDS. She also appeared in public service television ads sponsored by the American Medical Association, delivering humanitarian messages about AIDS patients.

Recognizing that, in her words, "Hispanics don't have access to the health information that they need," Lifshitz has successfully tapped into the mass media market as a way to convey her message and educate a larger audience. In 1986, she broadcast her first live call-in program on a southern California television station. After the program, Lifshitz received hundreds of calls and spent her entire weekend answering mail. The experience showed her how hungry people are for information. She began to appear regularly as a health commentator for the Spanish-language television station **Univision**, and produce prime time specials on health-related topics.

Lifshitz also began to reach out to her audience through the print media. She became the editor-in-chief of the magazine *Hispanic-Physician,* and the medical editor of *Mas,* a national Spanish-language magazine.

Aliza Lifshitz

Lifshitz believes strongly that women's health issues will become more prominent as more women enter the medical profession. To assist young Latina mothers, she has also written a book, *Healthy Mother, Healthy Baby,* the first bilingual book on prenatal care.

89. Ileana Ros-Lehtinen
(1952–)

Ileana Ros-Lehtinen

The first Cuban-American to serve in the United States Congress, **Ileana Ros-Lehtinen** is known for her fiery opposition to Cuban leader **Fidel Castro**. It is a passion born of personal experience.

Ros-Lehtinen was born in Havana, Cuba. When she was seven years old, her family fled to America after Castro's Communist revolution. For awhile, Ros-Lehtinen's father worked with other Cuban refugees to topple Castro; however, he later gave up on the idea and focused his attention on raising his children as patriotic Americans. Her father's passion for politics rubbed off on her, and later he became one of her closest political advisors.

Ros-Lehtinen studied at Florida International University, where she earned a bachelor's degree in 1975 and a master's degree in 1987. She later took courses toward her Ph.D. in education at the University of Miami. While she was pursuing her degrees, she founded a private elementary school, the **Eastern Academy**, where she worked as a teacher and administrator.

In 1982, Ros-Lehtinen was elected to the **Florida House of Representatives**, becoming the first Cuban-born woman to hold a seat in the Florida legislature. She served there for four years and subsequently moved up to the state senate. In 1989, she took another big step by running for the **U.S. Congress**. She won the seat in a controversial election tainted by racial tension.

Lee Atwater, the National Republican Party Chairman at the time, commented that he wanted her to win the seat because nearly half of the district was Hispanic. Her opponent, Democrat **Gerald Richman**, replied that it was "an American seat." Richman's comment offended Hispanics who interpreted it to mean they were somehow not American. Ros-Lehtinen captured the seat with 53 percent of the vote, becoming the first Cuban-American and the first Hispanic female to serve in Congress.

Ros-Lehtinen has been one of Congress's most vocal opponents of Castro. She spoke out against Cuba hosting the 1991 Pan American Games. She also objected to the popular reception given to South African leader Nelson Mandela when he visited Florida, because of his strong support for Castro. She also criticized what she believed was the Clinton administration's softening stance toward Castro.

While in Congress, Ros-Lehtinen has done more than crusade against Castro's government. She has been a crusader for tax reform, as well as a supporter of women's, Hispanic, and immigrant rights. She is also a vocal opponent of abortion, and she supports a constitutional amendment to ban flag burning.

Ros-Lentinen became so popular in her district, that she ran unopposed for reelection in the year 2000. She is married to Dexter Lehtinen, a former colleague in the Florida legislature, and they have two daughters.

Gary Soto was born and raised in Fresno, California. One of the first **Chicano writers** nominated for the **Pulitzer Prize,** his poetry reflects the pain and poverty of Mexican-American laborers in California's Central Valley.

Soto writes from experience. He grew up in a migrant laborer household, and when he was five years old, his father was killed in a work-related accident. As a young man, Soto, too, worked in the fields and factories around Fresno.

Soto studied at Fresno City College, where he initially majored in geography. He wanted to study maps because "he liked seeing the world in print," but he switched his major to poetry after reading Edward Field's poem "Unwanted." He recognized Field's feelings of social alienation and realized that it was something he, too, wanted to explore in his own writing.

In 1974, Soto graduated magna cum laude from California State University, Fresno, where he studied with the acclaimed poet **Philip Levine**. Soto earned his Master of Fine Arts degree three years later from the University of California at Irvine. After obtaining his degree, he took a teaching job in the English and Chicano Studies Departments of the University of California at Berkeley.

Soto's literary talents were apparent very early. He won a string of awards in the mid-1970s, while he was still a student. In 1978, his second book of poetry, *The Tale of Sunlight,* was nominated for the prestigious Pulitzer Prize as well as the National Book Award.

After Soto joined the faculty at UC Berkeley, he continued to write and win critical acclaim. In all, he has published more than a dozen books of poetry, fiction, and nonfiction, and he has won numerous honors, including the **Nation Discovery Prize** and a **Guggenheim Foundation Fellowship**.

Throughout his work, Soto describes the misery and despair of Mexican-American laborers. His style is sometimes lyrical and sometimes gritty, with an ironic and disdainful view of the American Dream.

Soto says, "I write because there is pain in my life, our family, and those living in the San Joaquin Valley. I write because those I work and live among can't write. I only have to think of the black factory worker I worked with in Los Angeles or the toothless farm laborer I hoed beside in the fields outside of Fresno. They are everything."

Gary Soto

Soto has said his ultimate goal is to be known as a writer who appeals to readers across the spectrum. He has continued to teach in Berkeley, and divides his time between there and Fresno.

Nydia Velázquez

Nydia Margarita Velázquez has accomplished numerous firsts as a public servant and **politician** in her native Puerto Rico and in the United States.

One of nine children, Velázquez was born in the town of Yabucoa. Her father worked as a sugar cane cutter, butcher, and local politician. Her mother sold *pasteles,* a local delicacy, to supplement the family income.

Velázquez became the first person in her family to receive a high school diploma, graduating at the age of 15. Although her family was poor, they possessed a passion for social issues, inspired by Nydia's father. As a result, after high school she enrolled at the University of Puerto Rico in Río Piedras to study political science.

Velázquez earned her bachelor's degree magna cum laude in 1974, and her master's degree from New York University in 1976. She then returned to Puerto Rico to teach political science at the University of Puerto Rico in Humacao.

In 1980, the New Progressive party won elections in Puerto Rico, and the pro-statehood ruling party took exception to Velázquez's pro-independence views. They accused her of being a Communist, and she returned to New York to avoid further criticism.

In 1981, Velázquez became an adjunct professor in Black and Puerto Rican Studies at New York's Hunter College. Two years later, she took a job working for Brooklyn Congressmen **Edolphus Towns** as special assistant for immigrant rights. In 1984, she was appointed to fill a vacancy on the **New York City Council,** becoming the first Latina to serve on the council. She failed in her bid for reelection two years later.

In 1986, Velázquez returned to Puerto Rico as director of the Department of Labor. Three years later, she was appointed to manage the Department of Puerto Rican Community Affairs in the United States. From her cabinet-level position, she initiated a Puerto Rican AIDS awareness campaign, and she led a drive to register more than 200,000 Puerto Rican voters in the Northeast and Midwestern United States.

In 1992, Velázquez was elected to the **U.S. Congress**, becoming the first Puerto Rican woman to serve there. It was a hard-fought victory in which she defeated an entrenched incumbent. She also overcame a public disclosure that she had attempted suicide a year earlier while battling depression over family problems.

In Congress, Velázquez has earned a reputation as a champion of labor and immigrants' rights, and an advocate of affordable housing. In 1998, she was named ranking Democrat on the **House Small Business Committee**, becoming the first Hispanic woman to serve as a ranking member of a full committee of the U.S. Congress.

92. Sandra Cisneros
(1954–)

A pioneer in **Chicana literature**, **Sandra Cisneros** draws upon her unique experiences as a poor Mexican-American woman growing up in two countries.

Born in Chicago to a working-class Mexican father and Mexican-American (Chicana) mother, she grew up the only daughter in a family with six sons. Her father was frequently homesick for Mexico, and would move the family back and forth between Mexico City and Chicago, which prevented Cisneros from making lasting friendships while growing up.

Cisneros was able to find an outlet in her solitude. She relied upon reading, writing, and her own imagination for creative expression. In high school, she became the editor of her school's literary magazine. After she earned her bachelor's degree from Loyola University in Chicago in 1976, she enrolled at the prestigious University of Iowa Writers' Workshop, where she earned her master's degree in fine arts in 1978.

While at Iowa, Cisneros realized that her unique experiences as a Mexican-American woman growing up in poverty provided her with the kind of material that set her writing apart from that of her peers.

In 1984, Cisneros published *The House on Mango Street*. The book is a collection of loosely connected stories told by Esperanza Cordero, a Mexican- American girl growing

Sandra Cisneros

up in a Chicago barrio. Like the author, the narrator struggles with internal conflicts of loneliness, poverty, and alienation. It is Cisneros's best-known work, and it drew praise for its poetic language and fresh perspective on the lives of poor Mexican-American women.

Although Cisneros has received critical acclaim for her work, at times she has struggled to earn a living as a writer. After she published her first book of poetry, *My Wicked Wicked Ways*, in 1987, she ran out of money and could not find work. She tried to start her own private writing workshops, but the venture was unsuccessful. She then moved from Texas and took a job teaching at California State University, Chico.

Since then, Cisneros has written other books of prose and poetry. In 1991, she published *Women Hollering Creek and Other Stories*, a collection of short stories about strong Mexican-American women living along the Texas-Mexico border. The contract she received from Random House made her the first Mexican-American woman to receive a major publishing contract for a work about Chicanas.

In addition to teaching at Cal State Chico, Cisneros has taught at other universities, including the University of California at Berkeley, University of California at Irvine, and the University of Michigan at Ann Arbor.

María Elena Durazo overcame an upbringing in severe poverty to become a pioneering **labor leader** in the city of Los Angeles.

Durazo was raised among migrant farmworkers in California. She and her nine brothers and sisters often worked in the fields with their parents, and at night they slept in the back of the family pickup truck.

After attending high school, Durazo worked her way through the Los Angeles People's College of Law. Inspired by the Chicano civil rights movement of the 1970s, she also began volunteering her time as an advocate for immigrants' rights. In 1979, she got her first paying job, as a labor organizer with the **International Ladies Garment Workers Union.** Later, she went to work for **Hotel and Restaurant Employees** (HERE) Local 11 in Los Angeles.

María Elena Durazo

When Durazo went to work for HERE, the local leadership was composed of mostly older, retired Anglos, who had grown out-of-touch with the rank-and-file membership, which was by then more than 70 percent Hispanic. A large number of the Hispanic members were immigrants from Mexico and Central American countries, and many of them spoke only Spanish. In spite of this, the leadership continued to conduct meetings and print publications only in English. Over time, the local lost half of its membership, and it ceased to be an effective labor organization.

In 1987, Durazo put together a slate of candidates to challenge the leadership. However, the election was tarnished by accusations of irregularities, and the international union declared a trusteeship. Two years later, the trusteeship ended, and Durazo put herself and her 15-person slate up for election again. This time she and all her allies won, with over 80 percent of the votes. The victory made her the first woman, and the first Hispanic woman, ever to run a major union in Los Angeles.

As president, she has implemented numerous changes, including conducting meetings in English and Spanish, and holding regular training sessions for members about how to negotiate their contracts with employers. Her policies resulted in an increase in membership and greater bargaining power, which led to improvements in the working conditions for thousands of cooks, dishwashers, and housekeepers in Los Angeles's huge hotel and restaurant industry. In 1998, the union won a groundbreaking contract for its members that included a 36 percent pay increase and a guaranteed right-of-return to their jobs for members who have problems with their immigration status.

In 1996, Durazo was also elected to the **National Executive Board** of HERE, becoming the first Hispanic woman to serve in that capacity. In 2001, she was honored by California Lieutenant Governor Cruz Bustamante, who chose her as the Lieutenant Governor's Woman of the Year.

94. Nancy Lopez
(1957–)

One of the greatest athletes in the history of women's golf, **Nancy Lopez** showed her extraordinary talents even before she was out of elementary school.

Born in Torrance, California, Lopez was raised in Roswell, New Mexico, where her family moved when she was a child. She was introduced to golf as a young girl, accompanying her parents on the course.

Lopez first started competing in tournaments, and winning them, when she was only nine years old. At 11, she could beat her father, who was also her coach. When she was 12 years old, she won the Women's State Amateur Tournament.

In high school, Lopez played on the school's previously all-male golf team. She was the team's best player and led them to the state championship. When she was 18 years old, she entered the **U.S. Women's Open** as an amateur and finished second.

Lopez enrolled in college, but left when she was 19 to turn professional. In 1978, her first year on the women's professional tour, she won the Bent Tree Classic in Florida, and after that, five more tournaments in succession. Her victories included the coveted **LPGA title**, which she later won twice more during her career.

Lopez's first-year successes earned her the LPGA titles of **Rookie of the Year** and **Player of the Year**, as well as the Associated Press's **Female Athlete of the Year**. From her tournament victories, she earned more than $200,000, which set a new record for women golfers.

The following year, 1979, Lopez entered 22 tournaments. She placed in the top 10 in 18 contests and won 8 of them.

In 1982, Lopez married major league baseball player **Ray Knight**, and in 1983 she took time off for maternity leave. Shortly after the birth of their daughter Ashley, she returned to the golf course. In 1985, she won five tournaments, set a record for low scoring average for the year, and earned more than $400,000 in prize money. She also won her second LPGA Player of the Year award and was once again named Associated Press Female Athlete of the Year.

Two years later, Lopez was inducted into the **LPGA Hall of Fame**, the youngest woman ever to receive that honor. In 1988, she became the fourth woman golfer to surpass $2 million in career earnings; in 22 tournaments that year, she had 3 victories, and finished in the top 5 on 12 occasions. The next year she won her third LPGA championship.

Lopez continued her career during the late 1980s, despite giving birth to two more daughters. During the 1990s, she gradually decreased her time on the course as she devoted more time to her family.

Nancy Lopez

Gloria Estefan
(1958–)

Gloria Estefan's singing career has made her one of America's greatest pop stars and one of music's most successful crossover artists.

She was born Gloria Fajardo in Havana, Cuba in 1958. Her family was staunchly anti-Castro. Her father, José Manuel Fajardo, was a soldier and a bodyguard for the Cuban dictator, Fulgencio Batista. When Fidel Castro 's Communists overthrew Batista's government in 1959, the Fajardo family, like most Batista supporters, fled to the United States.

José Fajardo later fought as a U.S. soldier in the Vietnam War. Shortly after his return from Vietnam, he developed multiple sclerosis, a disease of the nervous system. Gloria cared for her ailing father while her mother worked. She began singing as a form of emotional release during the long hours she spent at home.

Gloria Estefan

She earned her degree in psychology from the University of Miami in 1978, but by this time, she had already embarked on a professional singing career. While in college, she had joined the group **Miami Latin Boys**, led by **Emilio Estefan**, who became her husband a few years later.

The group originally performed songs only in Spanish and had several hits in Spanish-speaking countries. Eventually, the group changed its name to **Miami Sound Machine**; during the 1980s, they recorded their first crossover albums, "Eyes of Innocence" and "Primitive Love," which both featured songs in Spanish and English. With Estefan's husband working feverishly behind the scenes as the group's manager, Miami Sound Machine eventually signed a contract with the CBS/Sony label. The contract allowed the group to remain bilingual.

The group's song "Dr. Beat" was a hit in Europe, and in 1986, they had a world-wide sensation with the song "Conga." With their unique blend of Afro-Cuban rhythms and sounds combined with English lyrics, both songs appealed to a broad audience. When a producer complained that the group's music was "too Latin for the Americans and too American for the Latins," Estefan took it as a compliment. She exclaimed, "That's exactly what we are!"

In 1990, the band's bus was involved in an accident while on tour in Pennsylvania. Estefan broke her back and was temporarily paralyzed. She worked hard to recover, and miraculously, in 1991, she was able to join the band on a world tour.

Throughout the 1990s, Estefan continued to perform with the Miami Sound Machine, although she also embarked on a successful solo career. With her husband as her manager, she has sold nearly 100 million records worldwide.

The first Hispanic woman in space did not grow up with dreams of becoming an **astronaut**.

Ellen Ochoa was born in 1958 in Los Angeles and grew up in the town of La Mesa in San Diego County. She was a high achiever, and graduated as the valedictorian of her class at Grossmont High School in 1975.

In college, at California State University, San Diego, Ochoa changed her major five times before finally choosing physics. It proved to be an excellent choice, as she graduated again as the valedictorian of her class, in 1980, and went on to earn her master's degree in engineering from Stanford University in 1981.

While she was in graduate school, a number of Ochoa's friends applied for jobs at the **National Aeronautics and Space Administration** (NASA). This sparked her interest, and she eventually decided that she too wanted to join NASA—to become an astronaut. After she earned her doctorate in electrical engineering from Stanford in 1985, Ochoa first took a job on the technical staff in the Imaging Technology Division at Sandia National Laboratories in Livermore, California.

About this time, Ochoa's brother had received his pilot's license, and he encouraged her to do the same. She got her license, and in 1988 she went to work at NASA's **Ames Research Center** at Moffett Field, near San Jose, California. Within six months, she had been promoted to Chief of the Intelligent Systems Technology Branch, where she worked on optical recognition systems for space automation.

In 1990, Ochoa took the next step toward fulfilling her ambition when she was selected to train to become an astronaut. She went through a year of intensive training before qualifying in July 1991.

In April 1993, Ochoa joined the flight crew of the space shuttle *Discovery* and made history as the first Latina ever to fly into outer space. Her job on the mission was to use a robotic arm to deploy and retrieve a 2,800-pound satellite that conducted atmospheric and solar studies, including gathering important information about the sun's corona, the outermost part of the sun's atmosphere. The trip lasted more than nine days.

Ellen Ochoa

In November 1994, Ochoa made a second trip into space, as the payload commander aboard the space shuttle *Atlantis*. During this 11-day flight, she conducted more solar studies, focusing on the sun's energy and the effect it has on the earth's atmosphere.

Since the *Atlantis* mission, Ochoa has continued to work for NASA on robotics and space station research and development. She has every intention of going back into space, with hopes of living on a space station or someday joining a journey to Mars.

97. Loretta Sanchez
(1960–)

Loretta Sanchez became a symbol of the growing political power of Hispanics in the United States when, in 1996, she won a seat in **Congress** by defeating longtime incumbent California Representative **Robert Dornan**.

Born in Lynwood, California, Sanchez attended Chapman University. She then earned her master's degree in business administration from American University in Washington, D.C., in 1984. She returned to California and went to work as a financial analyst. In 1994, she entered politics and ran unsuccessfully for a seat on the Anaheim City Council.

Loretta Sanchez

The area where Sanchez lived and worked—**Orange County**—was known for many years as one of the most politically conservative counties in the country. Home to Disneyland and numerous middle and upper-class suburbs, most of its residents were white, and voted Republican. Beginning in 1984, Bob Dornan had been elected to represent California's 46th District, and had been reelected five times. He was a fiery, sometimes outrageous spokesperson for the conservative values that predominated in the district.

However, Orange County underwent numerous changes during the 1980s and '90s. As more immigrants entered southern California, Hispanics surpassed whites as the majority ethnic population in the county; it was no longer the homogenous, Republican stronghold it had once been. By the mid-1990s, Democrats held an eight-percent advantage over Republicans in the number of registered voters.

In 1996, Sanchez, the young business-woman with minimal political experience, ran as a Democrat against Dornan in the general election. Even with the changes that had occurred in the district, given the county's history and the huge advantage Dornan held as a five-time incumbent, most observers considered him unbeatable. On election day, it seemed the experts had been correct when Dornan appeared to have a 233-vote margin of victory. However, when absentee ballots were counted, Sanchez emerged the victor by 974 votes.

A stubborn and gutsy fighter, Dornan refused to concede. He charged the Sanchez campaign with voter fraud, accusing her of stealing the election with votes from noncitizens. The Orange County Registrar of Voters recounted the votes and confirmed Sanchez as the winner. The California Secretary of State's Office and the House of Representatives conducted investigations, both of which discounted Dornan's charges.

Refusing to accept that the Orange County voters had finally rejected him, Dornan challenged Sanchez 's bid for reelection in 1998. This time, she won by a lopsided 17 percent of the votes. In Congress, she became a member of both the **Armed Services** and the **Education and the Workforce committees**. In the 2000 election, Sanchez won a third term in the House, getting more than 62 percent of the vote.

Born and raised in San Pedro de Macoris, Dominican Republic, **Sammy Sosa** rose from poverty to become one of America's most celebrated sports heroes.

Sosa grew up in a single-parent household. His mother raised him, his four brothers, and two sisters after her husband died. The family was so poor that as a young boy, Sosa worked as a janitor, sold oranges, and shined shoes to help support the family.

Sosa's first love was boxing, but one of his brothers convinced him to try baseball. They played their own brand of baseball in the streets, using a rolled up sock for a ball and sticks for bats. Often Sosa played in his bare feet.

In 1985, when Sosa was 16 years old, a professional scout for the major league's **Texas Rangers** invited him to a tryout in Puerto Plata, a five-hour bus ride from his hometown. Although he was short and lanky with little baseball experience, at the tryout the scout saw his athletic potential. He signed Sosa for $3,500.

The next year, although he spoke no English, Sosa moved to the United States, to play in the Rangers' farm system. Within three years, he was playing in the major leagues. In 1989, the Rangers traded him to the **Chicago White Sox.**

Sosa played well in 1990, his first full season, but not so well in 1991, and the White Sox traded him to the crosstown **Chicago Cubs**. He improved steadily over the next several years, and by the late 1990s, he had become one of the premiere players in baseball.

In 1998, Sosa and St. Louis Cardinal slugger **Mark McGwire**, chased the ultimate record—**Roger Maris's** single-season home run mark of 61. Throughout the long season, Sosa and McGwire engaged in a home run

Sammy Sosa

duel that caught the imagination of baseball fans around the country. Ultimately, both of them broke the record; McGwire ended the season with 70 home runs, and Sosa finished with 66. That season, Sosa led the Cubs into the playoffs, and was voted the **National League's Most Valuable Player.**

Over the next three years, Sosa continued to put up great numbers, breaking the 60 home run mark in 1999 and again in 2001, becoming the first player in history to surpass 60 homes runs three times. He also became one of baseball's most popular players; with a winning smile and an exuberance for the game, he became a fan favorite both inside and outside of Chicago.

Sosa has used his financial success and popularity to become a humanitarian, providing financial support for schools and hospitals in his native country.

In her short life and career, **Selena** became a singing sensation and one of the leaders in the rising popularity of **Tejano music**. She was on the verge of national stardom when she died tragically—murdered at the age of 23.

Selena

Selena Quintanilla was born in Lake Jackson, Texas. Her father, a former singer, recognized her singing talent when she was only six years old; soon, she was giving her first public performance at her father's Tex-Mex restaurant. A short time later, she and her siblings formed a band, **Selena y Los Dinos** (Selena and the Boys), which began traveling and performing throughout southern Texas.

Selena made her first recording in 1979, and she left school in the eighth grade so she could spend more time traveling with her band. When she was 15 years old, she won **Tejano Music Awards** for best female vocalist and performer of the year. Two years later, the band signed a record deal with the Latin division of the EMI Records Group. In 1992, she married the band's guitarist, **Chris Pérez**.

Traditionally, Tejano meant music by Texans of Mexican descent, but Selena and others helped popularize the style by mixing in sounds of pop, country and western, and Caribbean music. She added her own sex appeal in the early 1990s, when she became known as the **"Tex-Mex Madonna"** for her bustiers and provocative looks.

In 1993, her recording, "Selena Live" received a **Grammy Award** for best Mexican-American album. Her next album, "Amor Prohibido," sold 600,000 copies in the United States. It featured the single "Fotos y Recuerdos," which reached the top ten on Billboard Magazine's Latino charts. By 1995, her albums had sold a total of three million copies.

That same year, Selena played to record crowds in Houston, and she dominated the Tejano Music Awards ceremonies. With appearances in American movies and on a Latino television soap opera, she seemed destined for a second career in acting.

In March of 1995, Selena went to confront the manager of her fan club, Yolanda Saldivar, whom she suspected of stealing money from the club. Saldivar met Selena at the door of her motel room and shot her in the back and shoulder. Selena died a few hours later.

The reaction to her death was a testament to Selena's popularity. Fifteen hundred mourners attended a vigil held before her funeral. Thousands came to see her coffin, and in cities like Los Angeles and San Antonio, thousands more gathered to pay their respects.

In 1997, the popular movie, *Selena,* depicted her life story—from the startling rise of her career, through its many succeses, to its tragic end.

100. Oscar De La Hoya
(1973–)

Oscar De La Hoya has said that he fights "first for my mother, then my family, then myself, then for all the people who support me—the Mexican people, all Hispanic people."

He was born in East Los Angeles, where his parents had relocated from Mexico. It was a relatively safe neighborhood, but gangs lurked nearby. He managed to avoid them because of his involvement in boxing.

Most of the men in De La Hoya's family were boxers. When he was six, his father gave him lessons. He knocked out his very first opponent, and his father knew he had a gifted fighter on his hands.

As a teenager, De La Hoya won the national **Junior Olympic championships**, the national **Golden Gloves** title, and the U.S. Amateur Boxing tournament. In 1990, he won a gold medal at the Goodwill Games.

In 1992, as the favorite to win the gold medal at the Summer Olympics in Barcelona, Spain, De La Hoya suffered a devastating loss when his mother passed away from breast cancer. He managed to overcome his grief and won the gold medal in the lightweight division.

After his Olympic victory, De La Hoya turned professional. Over the course of seven years, in 31 bouts, he amassed an undefeated record, beating such notables as **Julio Cesar Chavez**, **Pernell Whitaker**, and **Hector Camacho**. Along the way, he also captured the title in three different weight classes: super lightweight, lightweight, and welterweight. As his victories and titles mounted, De La Hoya became known as the **Golden Boy**, known for his fast hands, handsome looks, and sharp verbal skills with sportswriters.

In September 1999, De La Hoya, holder of the World Boxing Council's welterweight title, fought International Boxing Federation welterweight champion Felix Trinidad, in a title unification fight. De La Hoya lost a 12-round decision, his first professional defeat.

He lost for only the second time, in a bout against Shane Mosley, in June 2000.

In 2001, De La Hoya returned to the ring, and in June that year he defeated Spain's **Javier Castillejo** to capture the **WBC super welterweight crown**, winning his fourth title in as many weight classes. De La Hoya credits a new trainer, **Clarence Mayweather, Sr.**, with giving him the push to regain his championship form. "He trains me harder, shows me more defense," De La Hoya has said.

In spite of his triumphs, De La Hoya has had his share of critics. Some Mexcian-American fans feel he has forgotten his community roots because of his success. However, De La Hoya has donated money to several charities and spoken to schools in his old neighborhood on many occasions.

Oscar De La Hoya

Trivia Quiz & Projects

Test your knowledge and challenge your friends with the following questions. The answers are contained in the biographies noted.

1. Which 18th century Spanish priest established the first Catholic missions up and down the coast of present-day California? (see no. 4)
2. Which naval officer became a hero during the American Civil War by shouting the famous cry, "Damn the torpedoes! Full speed ahead!"? (see no. 10)
3. How did a 19th century Spanish-born architect create a series of spectacular buildings in the eastern United States? (see no. 17)
4. Who spent 60 years of her life as an activist, author, and radio and television host fighting for the rights of Hispanic-Americans? (see no. 24)
5. Which outstanding stage and film star won numerous honors for a career that spanned more than six decades? (see no. 32)
6. How did a Puerto Rican native transform her early childhood experience with labor struggles into a lifetime of service to poor and uneducated Puerto Ricans? (see no. 42)
7. Where did the most respected figure in the Hispanic-American civil rights movement organize the first U.S. farmworkers' union? (see no. 47)
8. Why is a Cuban-born playwright who immigrated to the United States when she was 15-years old called the "Picasso of theater"? (see no. 54)
9. Which native Puerto Rican baseball star rose to become one of the greatest players of all time? (see no. 61)
10. How did one of America's most successful pop-folk-singers also become an outspoken political activist? (see no. 69)
11. Why did a childhood experience with illness cause a Puerto Rican immigrant to make a commitment to a lifelong career in medicine and public health? (see no. 76)
12. When did a famous guitarist responsible for creating the music known as Latin rock reemerge as a top recording artist and performer? (see no. 83)
13. Which female tennis player was a pioneer and a rebel who helped make lasting changes to her sport? (see no. 85)
14. How does a California Chicano poet use his life experiences to write about the plight of Mexican-American laborers? (see no. 90)
15. Which Cuban-born singer has become one of America's greatest pop stars and one of music's most successful crossover artists? (see no. 95)
16. How did a native of the Dominican Republic rise from poverty to become one of America's most famous sports heroes? (see no. 98)

Suggested Projects
1. Choose one of the people from this book and write a one-page fictional diary entry for one day in that person's life. Pick a day that had some significance for the individual; for example, the day he or she was elected to public office, received a significant award, or achieved some other noteworthy success. Or choose a day on which the person met with a personal setback, or was frustrated in some way by a lack of success. Describe the person's thoughts and feelings with as much detail as you can.

2. Arrange a "meeting" of two of the people in this book who could never have met in real life. Choose two individuals from different eras and perhaps from even different walks of life. (For example, Junipero Serra and George Santayana or Sara Estela Ramírez and Romana Acosta Banuelos.) Imagine what their meeting would be like. Write 1-2 pages describing the scenario of their meeting, and create dialogue between the two people. What kinds of questions do you think they would ask each other? Would they approve of the things that each had done in their lifetimes? Be as imaginative as you can.

INDEX

Index

Index

Index

psychologist 78
publisher 28
Pueblo Indian 10
Puente, Tito 50, 51, 61
Puerto Rico 25, 49, 98
Pulitzer Prize 94, 97

Quinn, Anthony 39

Ramírez, Sara Estela 27
Ramona's Mexican Food
    Products 52
Reagan, Ronald 55
Reed, Walter 23
Republican party 21, 55,
    96, 104
Ridge, John Rollin 22
Rivera, Diego 69, 85
Rivera, Geraldo 80
Rodriguez, Richard 84
Rodriquez de Tió, Lola 25
Roman Catholic Church 9,
    10, 12, 15
Rondstadt, Linda 73
Roosevelt, Franklin D. 36
Ros-Lehtinen, Ileana 96
Royal Society of Literature
    (London) 26
Roybal, Edward 42
Roybal-Allard, Lucille 42,
    77

Saint Francis, Order of 11
Salazar, Reubén 57
salsa music 50, 51
San Diego, Bay of 11
San Francisco Presido 12,
    20
San Juan Bautista 1
San Juan de los
    Caballeros 10

Sanchez, Loretta 104
Santana, Carlos 90
Santayana, George 26
Saralegui, Cristina Maria
    93
scientist 55
Seguín, Juan N. 19, 87
Selena 106
Senate, California State 21
Senate, U.S. 21, 30
Serra, Junipero 11
Serrano, Lupe 64
settler 20
singer 29, 51, 73, 76, 86,
    91, 102, 106
Siqueiros, David Alfaro 85
Social and Public Art
    Resource Center
    (SPARC) 85
Sociedad de Obreros
    (Society of Workers)
    27
Sosa, Sammy 105
Soto, Gary 97
Southwest Voter
    Registration Education
    Project (SVREP) 81
Spanish Civil War 34
Spanish-American War 23
Surgeon General (U.S.) 83

Tejano music 106
Tejano Music Award 106
Tenayuca, Emma 41
theater, Chicano 74
Tijerina, Reies López 53,
    59
Tony Award 66, 88
Top Hispanic Designer 71
Treaty of Guadalupe
    Hidalgo 18

Trevino, Lee 72

House Un-American
    Activities Committee
    41
United Farm Workers
    Union (UFW) 44, 62
Universidad Boricua 49

Valdez, Luis 74
Vallejo (California) 20
Vallejo, Mariano
    Guadalupe 20
vault, Catalan 24
Velásquez, William C. 81
Velázquez, Nydia
    Margarita 98
Vietnam War 57, 76, 85,
    102
Villaseñor, Victor 75

War of 1812 14, 17
World War I 32
World War II 35, 36, 37,
    38, 40, 41, 42, 45, 46,
    47, 50
writer 25, 27, 31, 45, 59,
    61, 69, 75, 78, 84, 94,
    97, 99

yellow fever 23
Yglesias, José 45
Yuma Indians 12

Zapata, Carmen 56
Zorro 22